STRONGMAN'S

HIS NAME....

WHAT'S HIS GAME?

STRONGMAN'S

His Name....

What's His Game?

An Authoritative Biblical Approach to Spiritual Warfare

DRS. JERRY & CAROL ROBESON

WHITAKER HOUSE

STRONGMAN'S HIS NAME...WHAT'S HIS GAME?
An Authoritative Biblical Approach to Spiritual Warfare
new edition

Dr. Carol Robeson
Shiloh Publishing House
P.O. Box 100
Woodburn, OR 97071

ISBN-13: 978-0-88368-601-5
ISBN-10: 0-88368-601-0
Printed in the United States of America

WHITAKER HOUSE
1030 Hunt Valley Circle
New Kensington, PA 15068
www.whitakerhouse.com

Library of Congress Cataloging-in-Publication Data
Robeson, Jerry, 1938–1999.
Strongman's his name—what's his game? / by Jerry & Carol Robeson.
p. cm.
Originally published: Woodburn, OR : Shiloh Pub., © 1983.
ISBN 0-88368-601-5 (trade paper : alk. paper)
1. Spiritual warfare—Biblical teaching. I. Robeson, Carol, 1939- II. Title.
BS680.S73 .R64 2002
235'.4—dc21
2001056901

3 4 5 6 7 8 9 10 11 12 13 14 15 14 13 12 11 10 09 08 07

Preface

Most of us have seen the advertisement showing a ninety-eight-pound weakling getting sand kicked in his face by the huge beach bully. The muscle-bound loudmouth then walks off with the poor guy's girlfriend.

The next scene shows the discouraged young man starting a muscle-building program. He vows fervently that he will never be humiliated like that again.

After a few short months of intense exercise, we see that he has developed into a gorgeous specimen of manhood.

The last frame shows our hero delivering a well-aimed blow to the jaw of the bully with the appropriate caption, "Take that, you rat, and don't ever bother my girl again!"

On a spiritual level, God wants to turn you into a spiritual dynamo so that you can stand up to Satan, the bully of the universe, and tell him he can't take advantage of you.

Listen as Jesus tells us how we are to live now that He has defeated the Enemy.

> *And these signs shall follow them that believe; In my name shall they cast out devils; they shall speak with new tongues; they shall take up serpents; and if they drink any deadly thing, it shall not hurt them; they shall lay hands on the sick, and they shall recover.* (Mark 16:17–18)

This isn't saying that you will be *looking* for demons to attack. It simply means that you won't have to put up with being knocked around or confused by their disruptive activities. You will be able to nail them in their tracks when they pop their heads up and, as a result, live a victorious Christian life.

We are told that *"God hath not given us the spirit of fear; but of power, and of love, and of a sound mind"* (2 Timothy 1:7).

Isn't that what you want? Let us show you how you can be *"more than conquerors through him that loved us"* (Romans 8:37).

—Jerry and Carol Robeson

Table of Contents

Introduction

As children of God, we must understand that our heavenly Father is *good*. His chief goal in our lives is to make us the best people we can possibly be. Everything He does as He deals with us in our Christian lives is to develop our potential to the greatest degree possible.

On the other hand, Satan is totally evil. Jesus gave us Satan's job description in John 10:10, when He said, *"The thief cometh not, but for to steal, and to kill, and to destroy."*

To better understand who God is, let's look at the attributes and characteristics of God, which He has revealed about Himself in His Word.

Attributes of God

God Is:

1. Spirit
2. Holy—He has never been touched by sin.
3. Eternal—He has always existed.
4. Infinite—without limits except when He has limited Himself by His Word.
5. Omnipresent—everywhere at once.
6. Omniscient—all knowing.
7. Omnipotent—all mighty.
8. Truth—He never, ever lies.
9. Just—100 percent fair in His actions with us.
10. Righteous—totally good.
11. Life—He isn't just alive...He *is* Life.
12. Unchangeable—*"Every good gift and every perfect gift is from above, and comes down from the Father of lights, with whom there is no variation or shadow of turning"* (James 1:17).
13. Sovereign—absolute supreme ruler. But His sovereignty is in complete harmony with His other attributes. God never, ever steps out of character in any one of His attributes.
14. Love—He is the most loving personality in the universe.
15. Faithful—absolutely trustworthy.
16. Merciful—beyond human comprehension.
17. Provident—watches over and cares for His creation.

God's attributes never get out of balance with each other. He never acts out of character.

For this reason, we can trust and have confidence in God's judgment concerning our lives. He will *always* do what is best for us. He is totally wise, good, and just. His love for us is so great that it is beyond understanding, and He is absolutely trustworthy. So why would anyone ever want to disregard His leading and advice in their lives?

Now, what about the enemy? What does the Bible reveal about his character?

Attributes of the Devil

The Devil Is:

1. A liar
2. A murderer
3. A sower of discord
4. An adversary
5. Cunning
6. Wicked
7. Malignant—totally evil
8. Cowardly
9. A tempter
10. A thief
11. Without principles
12. Proud
13. Deceitful
14. Fierce and cruel
15. Aggressive
16. A destroyer

As we compare these two lists of attributes, who do you suppose causes sickness and suffering in the human race?

Understand that the devil is not a negative God, but a fallen angel. As a result of the fall, he did not become more powerful. Sin *always* weakens whatever it touches. Are we stronger or weaker after we have sinned? Just because he was Lucifer does not nullify the fact that he is nothing now compared to what he was when he was created perfect. However, if we get into the works of the flesh, he is powerful because that is his playground.

Some of the works of the devil are sin, sickness, fear, death, depression, murder, temptation, deception, lust, and rebellion. But 1 John 3:8 informs us, *"For this purpose the Son of God was manifested, that he might destroy the works of the devil."* Now, in the name of Jesus, we have victory over the devil and his works because Jesus made them of no effect.

God will never stoop so low as to use one of the works of the devil to deal with His children. God would not have sent Jesus to destroy the works of the devil only to pick them back up to use on those He loves. We can have confidence that God has enough wisdom to deal with us on a higher level than the devil would use.

Trust in the Lord

Many have unfairly attributed the devil's acts to God. The results are devastating. What can a person do if he believes it is God who sent sickness into his life to teach him something? He shouldn't fight against God, so he allows the sickness to rob him of his health when he should be standing against it in the name of Jesus to be healed. We have to be able to recognize who is doing what in our lives if we are going to be able to react correctly according to God's Word.

Open Doors

Now let's look at a very important truth in spiritual warfare. Paul told us that we are the determining factor in whether the devil can operate in our lives or not. He said, *"Neither give place to the devil."* Or, as the *Amplified Bible* says, *"Leave no room or foothold for the devil...give no opportunity to him"* (Ephesians 4:27). When we allow openings in our spiritual lives, the devil feels he has the right to take advantage of us in those specific territories. If we keep the doors closed, he can't do what he would like to do.

The Bible introduces us to the open door principle in Genesis 4:7, where the Lord said to Cain, *"If thou doest not well, sin lieth at the door. And unto thee shall be his desire, and thou shalt rule over him."*

God told Cain that Satan was crouched at his doorway, waiting to leap into his life. Cain had the choice, and because he chose to open the door to jealousy, Satan led him into the murder of his brother, Abel.

Sin is progressive. One thing leads to another until we find ourselves in big trouble. For that reason, we must learn to close those doors, and keep them closed, before they develop into something harmful.

What Are Open Doors?

Lineage

An area that we should examine closely is inherited weakness from our family lineage. Our ancestors may have done things we are completely unaware of that can still affect us today.

The first commandment concerning graven images carries this warning, *"Thou shalt not bow down thyself to them, nor serve them: for I the Lord thy God am a jealous God, visiting the iniquity of the fathers upon the children unto the third and fourth generation of them that hate me"* (Exodus 20:5). We'll be touching this in more detail later on, complete with a model prayer, so that you can shut this door if it should apply to your case.

Crisis

An emotional or physical crisis can leave doors open that we must go back and close so that the enemy will not continue to hassle us in that part of our lives.

Ignorance

Ignorance of the Word can leave openings in our defenses that are devastating. Paul warned believers six times *"not to be ignorant"* concerning the Word of God. If you don't know your rights as a child of God, how can you defend yourself?

After we have gotten up and dusted ourselves off for the umpteenth time, the questions usually come, "Where did *that* come from? Why is this happening to me? I thought when I got saved I would be protected from these kinds of things. What can I do to stop this vicious cycle?"

Let's go to God's Word and find the answers to those questions.

Put on Your Armor

Ephesians is our first stop:

> *Be strong in the Lord, and in the power of his might. Put on the whole armour of God, that ye may be able to stand against the wiles of the devil. For we wrestle not against flesh and blood, but against principalities, against powers, against the rulers of the darkness of this world, against spiritual wickedness in high places. Wherefore take unto you the whole armour of God, that ye may be able to withstand in the evil day, and having done all, to stand.*
>
> (Ephesians 6:10–13)

Recognize your enemy. Put on the armor of God. Don't sit around feeling sorry for yourself. Begin doing what you must do for yourself. (We're going to show you how to do this in later chapters.)

We see that it is not human personalities we are fighting. It is Satan himself, with all his henchmen.

Don't let this fact throw you, though. The promise of God is, *"Submit yourselves therefore to God. Resist the devil, and he will flee from you"* (James 4:7).

From there we go on to 2 Timothy 2:15, where we are instructed, *"Study to show thyself approved unto God, a workman that needeth not to be ashamed, rightly dividing the word of truth."* When we are grounded in God's Word and find ourselves in battle with the enemy, we will have no question about who we are fighting, what the procedure is to defeat him, and by whose authority we will gain the victory.

Hosea the prophet warned the Hebrews: *"My people are destroyed for lack of knowledge"* (Hosea 4:6). This is basic. Buy yourself a set of cassette tapes of the New Testament and listen to them instead of some of the other things you listen to. Find a church that preaches the Word of God and feeds your spirit.

Faith Is the Key

The reason we need such a church is because, *"Faith cometh by hearing, and hearing by the word of God"* (Romans 10:17). We can't get away from the Word because it is the cornerstone of our faith. Our power source is faith in the Lord Jesus Christ and His Word. When we fully understand this principle, we are ready to begin putting His instructions into practice.

> *Verily I say unto you, Whatsoever ye shall bind on earth shall be bound in heaven: and whatsoever ye shall loose on earth shall be loosed in heaven. Again I say unto you, That if two of you shall agree on earth as touching any thing that they shall ask, it shall be done for them of my Father which is in heaven. For where two or three are gathered together in my name, there am I in the midst of them.* (Matthew 18:18–20)

Can you see the power God gives us when we let our faith level rise through the hearing of the Word of God? As we go through this study, we'll see the importance of binding the enemy in the name of Jesus and loosing the power of the Holy Spirit. This does not mean that the Holy Spirit is tied up and needs to be loosed. When we loose, we release or invite the Holy Spirit to accomplish in us what the will of God is for our lives. God can only do what we allow Him to do. So, by an act of our wills we open ourselves up to Him so that He can freely work as He sees fit in our lives, families, or situations. Then, after the enemy has been kicked out of his stronghold and the breech has been repaired, we can keep him from ever gaining an advantage over us in that area again.

Our Part

Note that God doesn't do everything. There is a part that we must do.

> *The night is far spent, the day is at hand: **let us** therefore **cast off** the works of darkness, and **let us put on** the armour of light. **Let us walk honestly**, as in the day; not in rioting and drunkenness, not in chambering and wantonness, not in strife and envying. But **put ye on** the Lord Jesus Christ, and **make not provision** for the flesh, to fulfil the lusts thereof.*
> (Romans 13:12–14, emphasis added)

Positive action is required. Wake up, walk honestly, and put off the works of darkness. Remember that Paul was writing here to a Christian body of believers just like you and me. He was not writing to pagans. These believers were into the works of darkness. Some of them were still hanging on to past or pet sins. If that is the case in our lives, we must cast off those things that pull us down spiritually. Ask the Holy Spirit to show you where your weak areas are and start changing them with the help of the Lord.

Then we are to put on the armor of light and the Lord Jesus Christ as we would put on a garment. Don't start your day without making up your mind not to fulfill the desires and lusts of the flesh. Put on the holiness of Christ so you will not sin against God. That takes willpower. But when we will to act, God is then released to pour His power into our life so we can be overcomers.

The Strongman

Now here is a major truth we will be dealing with as we go through this study. *"How can one enter into a strong man's house, and spoil his goods, except he first bind the strong man? and then he will spoil his house"* (Matthew 12:29).

> *When a strong man armed keepeth his palace, his goods are in peace: but when a stronger than he shall come upon him, and overcome him, he taketh from him all his armour wherein he trusted, and divideth his spoils.* (Luke 11:21–22)

Who? What? How?

In these two parallel passages, Jesus called the demonic presence a "strongman." Who is the strongman? What is his name? What does he do?

Once we know the answers to those questions, we can zero in and bind him in the name of Jesus, forbidding him to come back to harass us again. Then, according to Matthew 18:18, we loose the power of God to fill our lives and repair the damage done by the strongman.

It is possible to spend hours binding symptoms. The mortal blow comes, however, when we sever the main root, or the strongman, who is energizing the activity. If we don't take care of it properly the first time, the problem will return. It is like a carrot. We don't occupy ourselves pulling all the little hair roots, we pull up the carrot and all the little hair roots come along with it or die from lack of nourishment.

In warfare, when the general surrenders, all the troops under his command automatically surrender with him. The same principle applies in spiritual warfare.

Jesus gave further light on this subject:

> *When the unclean spirit is gone out of a man, he walketh through dry places, seeking rest; and finding none, he saith, I will return unto my house whence I came out. And when he cometh, he findeth it swept and garnished. Then goeth he, and taketh to him seven other spirits more wicked than himself; and they enter in, and dwell there: and the last state of that man is worse than the first.* (Luke 11:24–26)

Follow-Up

Do you see that it wasn't enough to just bind the strongman and cast him out with all his belongings? Follow-up work was necessary. We must learn how to *maintain* the freedom God has given to us, whether it is a case of possession or just harassment. That will keep us from having to repeat the same hassles over and over again in our Christian lives. Some Christians never seem to get beyond a certain point in their spiritual lives. Whenever they arrive at a particular plateau, "something" seems to kick their spiritual legs out from under them, and they land back at square one again. After the "house" is cleaned by repentance of sin and rejection of satanic influences, we must then feed on the Word so that the "house" is transformed into the temple of the Holy Spirit.

Can Christians Be Possessed?

Don't misunderstand. It is not that we see demons everywhere and in everybody. *Not everything is caused by demons.* However, the point is that, when it *is* an evil influence that is operating, we will recognize it and deal with it according to God's Word.

We do *not* believe that Christians can be demon-possessed. But they certainly can be attacked in their minds, wills, emotions, and bodies. They can be troubled, pressed, buffeted, harassed, depressed, obsessed, oppressed, in bondage, and bruised. Those people who are in the final state of possession or are indwelt have long since severed their relationship with God. They may still hang on to a form of godliness, but it is only an empty shell camouflaging their true spiritual condition.

Although much of the problem in this area is a matter of semantics, it is still necessary to state some clear principles of what God's Word actually says about the matter. The following are some of those Scriptures that lead us to believe that blood-washed believers, living according to the Word of God and loving the Lord with all of their hearts, cannot be demon-possessed.

1. Matthew 6:24 and Luke 16:13 *"No man can serve two masters: for either he will hate the one, and love the other; or else he will hold to the one, and despise the other. Ye cannot serve God and mammon."*

It is true that *"mammon"* refers to riches in this verse, but the principle still remains true that it is either God or the devil that rules in our lives, not both at the same time. (Mammon was the demonic god of wealth and profit.)

2. James 3:11–12 *"Doth a fountain send forth at the same place sweet water and bitter? Can the fig tree, my brethren, bear olive berries? either a vine, figs? so can no fountain both yield salt water and fresh."*

3. 1 Corinthians 10:21 *"Ye cannot drink the cup of the Lord, and the cup of devils: ye cannot be partakers of the Lord's table, and of the table of devils."*

This has reference to the Lord's supper, but once again we see the principle that God will not share us with the devil under any circumstances.

4. 1 Corinthians 3:16–17 *"Know ye not that ye are the temple of God, and that the Spirit of God dwelleth in you? If any man defile the temple of God, him shall God destroy; for the temple of God is holy, which temple ye are."*

Can you imagine demons running around in God's holy temple? I can't!

5. 1 Corinthians 6:19 *"What? know ye not that your body is the temple of the Holy Ghost which is in you, which ye have of God, and ye are not your own?"*

Some believe that, under certain circumstances, demons can possess the soul and body of a Christian without violating the spirit. But this verse states that our *"**body** is the temple of the Holy Ghost"* (emphasis added), not of the devil. In any event, we are not some kind of condominium, with demons living in one or two rooms and God in the other. It is either one or the other.

6. 1 John 4:4 *"Ye are of God, little children, and have overcome them: because greater is he* [God] *that is in you, than he* [the devil] *that is in the world."*

John told us where the devil is if God is in us: he is *"in the world."* What we are really discussing when we wonder whether demons can possess a Christian is simply whether God is stronger than the devil. If we believe a demon can possess the very temple of God, then we have no faith in the fact that God's protection is complete when we serve Him with all our hearts.

7. 1 Corinthians 2:12 *"Now we have received, not the spirit of the world* [demonic], *but the spirit which is of God; that we might know the things that are freely given to us of God."*

8. 1 John 5:18 *"We know that whosoever is born of God sinneth not; but he that is begotten of God keepeth himself, and that wicked one toucheth him not."*

The Greek word for *"toucheth"* means to fasten, cling to, or attach oneself to. Here we are told that if we are not practicing sin (*Amplified Bible* and Spanish translation), the devil doesn't have a right to touch us.

Some Christians mistakenly attribute works of the flesh to demon possession. Our flesh has some strong ideas of how it wants to live. If we don't use the power of the Holy Spirit to keep it subdued, it can raise havoc.

Then there are others who would rather have demons cast out of them than personally have to deal with their flesh and keep it on the altar of sacrifice as Romans 12:1 commands: *"I beseech you therefore, brethren, by the mercies of God, that ye present your bodies a living sacrifice, holy, acceptable unto God, which is your reasonable service."*

It is not God's will for His children to live in constant bondage.

"If the Son therefore shall make you free, ye shall be free indeed" (John 8:36). That is the reason we have taken the time to do this study. We want you to know that God has provided complete liberty for you over the enemy. We have power over the forces of hell when they attack us or members of our families.

Paul

Paul didn't beat around the bush. He told us who it is we are fighting. *"Put on the whole armour of God, that ye may be able to stand against the wiles of the devil"* (Ephesians 6:11).

A lot of people would like to believe that it is just the evil days in which we live or negative influences that cause our spiritual problems. No, we must be more specific than that. We are fighting an adversary, and his name is Satan.

Peter

Peter called him by name. *"Be sober, be vigilant; because your adversary the devil, as a roaring lion, walketh about, seeking whom he may devour: whom resist stedfast in the faith"* (1 Peter 5:8–9).

James

James comforted us when he told us to *"resist the devil, and he will flee from you"* (James 4:7). This is a picture of what happens in the spirit world when we walk in the authority of God's Word and use the name of Jesus. Satan and his demons have to obey. They don't have a choice in the matter! They begin to tremble and run when we speak according to God's Word.

So as you study, keep in mind that it is God's will for you to be free from every evil influence of the devil. He wants you to be free to enjoy all the good things He has prepared for His children. He promises us salvation, peace, joy, health, protection, provision, wisdom, and eternal life to name just a few. Take what you need from the Word of God so that you will never again be robbed of God's very best in your life.

Remember, *"though we walk in the flesh, we do not war after the flesh: (For the weapons of our warfare are not carnal, but mighty through God to the pulling down of strong holds;) casting down imaginations, and every high thing that exalteth itself against the knowledge of God, and bringing into captivity every thought to the obedience of Christ"* (2 Corinthians 10:3–5).

In our study of God's Word, we have found that there are at least sixteen strongmen mentioned by name. We will study them one by one and show you how they like to operate and their symptoms on the tree diagrams. Just as a doctor diagnoses disease by pinpointing the symptoms presented by the patient, you will recognize symptoms or manifestations or minor spirits of the strongman so that you can know exactly where the devil is coming from. Then, instead of making stabs in the dark when you are under attack by the enemy, you will know immediately who is trying to hassle you or members of your family and also how you can resist and drive them away according to biblical teaching.

Spirit of Divination

Acts 16:16–18

<u>Fortune-teller, Soothsayer</u>

Micah 5:12; Isaiah 2:6

<u>Warlock/Witch, Sorcerer</u>

Exodus 22:18

<u>Stargazer—Zodiac, Horoscopes</u>

Isaiah 47:13; Leviticus 19:26; Jeremiah 10:2

<u>Drugs (Greek, pharmakos)</u>

Galatians 5:20; Revelation 9:21; 18:23; 21:8; 22:15

<u>Rebellion</u>

1 Samuel 15:23

<u>Hypnotist, Enchanter</u>

Deuteronomy 18:11; Isaiah 19:3

<u>Water Witching</u>

Hosea 4:12

<u>Magic</u>

Exodus 7:11; 8:7; 9:11

Roots are
"...works of the flesh."
—Galatians 5:19–21

"By their fruits ye shall know them."
—Matthew 7:20

According to Matthew 18:18...

Bind: Spirit of Divination

Loose: Holy Spirit and Gifts

1 Corinthians 12:9–12

CHAPTER 1

Spirit of Divination

The dictionary defines *divination* as, "the practice of attempting to foretell future events or discover hidden knowledge by occult or supernatural means."[1]

God's Word goes a step further by showing that people who divine are controlled or possessed by supernatural spirits that enable them to receive information beyond the human realm. God's prophets receive their divine revelation by the Holy Spirit. On the other side of the spectrum are demonic spirits feeding information to fortune-tellers and sorcerers.

PAUL

Luke told us of such a case in the book of Acts.

> *And it came to pass, as we went to prayer, a certain damsel possessed with a spirit of divination met us, which brought her masters much gain by soothsaying: the same followed Paul and us, and cried, saying, These men are the servants of the most high God, which show unto us the way of salvation. And this did she many days. But Paul, being grieved, turned and said to the spirit, I command thee in the name of Jesus Christ to come out of her. And he came out the same hour.* (Acts 16:16–18)

The girl was a known fortune-teller, or soothsayer, in the community. Although she spoke the truth about Paul and his party, it was not her intent to help them through her proclamations. The very fact that a woman of her reputation would choose to advertise their ministry was a terrible reproach to the name of Jesus.

As Paul became more and more grieved in his spirit, the Holy Spirit revealed what was going on, and he rebuked the spirit of divination in the name of Jesus Christ.

NOTES

NOTES

God works through His children against the power of evil.

He didn't speak to the girl but to the spirit that was operating through her.

We have a clear example here that the power of God is always greater than the power of the devil. *"Greater is he that is in you, than he that is in the world"* (1 John 4:4). The demon had to leave when it was ordered to do so in the name of Jesus by a child of God.

God Wants You!

It also reveals that God wants to work through His children *against* the power of evil. The battle of the universe is God against the devil, good against evil, and we must choose which side we prefer. It is impossible to dabble with both powers at the same time. God's Word thunders down through the ages, *"Come out from among them, and be ye separate, saith the Lord,...for what fellowship hath righteousness with unrighteousness? and what communion hath light with darkness?"* (2 Corinthians 6:17, 14).

One of the problems today is that many Christians are unaware of where the dividing line is between the things of God and Satan's territory. When God's people stray into those areas that appear harmless but in reality are demonic, it creates all kinds of havoc in their spiritual lives.

Let's begin by showing what we must stay clear of as far as divination is concerned so we can live the kind of life that pleases God.

Mechanical Props

The spirit of divination often makes use of mechanical props such as sand, bones, entrails of a sacrifice, tea leaves, tarot cards, lines on the palm, horoscopes, lumps on the head, Ouija boards, planchets, crystal balls, occult computer games, charms, and drugs, etc. It also often uses magic, levitation, water witching, automatic writing, occult literature or objects, and handwriting analysis.

And what does God say about these things? He says:

> *Therefore hearken not ye to your prophets, nor to your diviners, nor to your dreamers, nor to your enchanters, nor to your sorcerers, which speak unto you, saying, Ye*

shall not serve the king of Babylon: for they prophesy a lie unto you, to remove you far from your land.
(Jeremiah 27:9–10)

And they left all the commandments of the LORD their God, and made them molten images, even two calves, and made a grove, and worshipped all the host of heaven, and served Baal. And they caused their sons and their daughters to pass through the fire, and used divination and enchantments, and sold themselves to do evil in the sight of the LORD, to provoke him to anger. (2 Kings 17:16–17)

Notes

Why God Hates Divination

God hates divination because it leads people to seek satanic intelligence for guidance in their lives instead of God and His Word. We cannot mix the guidance of the Holy Spirit with that of Satan without getting into problems. Millions of people in our world are doing just that when they consult their horoscopes instead of God's Word for their daily direction.

Horoscopes

When you pin many of these people down, they get a silly little grin on their faces and quickly tell you it is only a harmless game. One person told me that nobody really gets too serious about horoscopes. It's just fun to see if anything comes true. Later, I found that it was a much more serious problem area in this person's life than "just fun."

A few years ago, I picked up a *Miami Herald* newspaper with the headline blaring, "32 Million, Mostly Women, Believe in Astrology and Let It Run Their Lives."

The Gallup Poll went on to state that, "One in four adults reads an astrology column regularly and believes their life is governed by the position of the stars.

"The survey shows that almost as many churchgoers as non-churchgoers believe in astrology.

"One of the most surprising findings was that nearly eight in ten Americans (nine in ten under thirty years old) can name the sign under which they were born."[2]

Notes

Only a loving Father can give us direction.

My Survey

In a survey I made while speaking in ladies' religious meetings, I asked the question, "How many of you are now involved in horoscopes or other occult practices, or were involved before you were saved and did not know that you should renounce any connection with those occult practices even after accepting Christ?"

I estimated that 90 percent of the women raised their hands. Mind you, I wasn't speaking to followers of Satan. These were Christian ladies who had either left a wide-open door because of their past actions or were still dabbling in it after accepting Christ!

When we reach out beyond God's provision for us, we are in danger of hooking into demonic knowledge. Can we really take that chance?

Demon spirits cannot be relied upon for guidance. They mix their limited knowledge with lies to hold people's attention. Their brand of guidance leads their followers downward as they are slowly sucked into the whirlpool of evil. Only a loving Father can give us the direction we need today.

Creation versus Creator

> *Let now the astrologers, the stargazers, the monthly prognosticators, stand up, and save thee from these things that shall come upon thee. Behold, they shall be as stubble; the fire shall burn them; they shall not deliver themselves from the power of the flame.*
>
> (Isaiah 47:13–14)

Deuteronomy 18:12 informs us that one of the reasons God drove the nations out from before the Israelites was because of the sin of divination. Maybe those nations started out studying the stars as a pastime. But over a period of time it became more and more of a fascination to them until, in the final stages, they worshipped and served *"creature more than the Creator, who is blessed for ever"* (Romans 1:25).

Ur of Chaldea had its moon god worship. Abraham had to be called out of it before God could begin using him.

The tower of Babel was an apparent attempt to study the heavens so that the people could become like gods themselves. God interrupted it before it got out of hand.

The ancient Egyptians had their sun god worship and they were overthrown. All down through history, the nations and people who became involved in occult worship were destroyed.

Fortune-Tellers

Not long after we moved to a small town in Oregon, we noticed that a fortune-teller had established a place of business directly across from a Christian bookstore we often visited. We agreed together with the owner and manager that each time we looked in the fortune-teller's direction or passed in front of the building, we would curse it in the name of Jesus and bind the spirit of divination involved there.

A week or so later, a rival group of fortune-tellers broke all the windows in the building and, shortly after, the place was empty. Praise the Lord!

We are warned to stay away from fortune-tellers or, as the Bible calls them, soothsayers and seers.

"I will cut off witchcrafts out of thine hand; and thou shalt have no more soothsayers" (Micah 5:12).

People who put their trust in this kind of practice are usually full of confusion, problems, fears, misunderstandings, hatred, bitterness, unbreakable habits, and calamity because that is the end result of such satanic practices.

Hypnotists, Charmers, Passive Mind States

Charmers or chanters today would be labeled hypnotists. Hypnotism is big business now. We are inundated with commercials telling about people who have stopped smoking or lost weight through hypnosis. Some dentists and doctors use it to control their patients' pain. Other individuals use self-hypnosis to help them concentrate or sleep at night.

But don't be fooled. Just because the initial benefits may be positive does not mean that the long-range results will be the same.

Notes

NOTES

Never allow anyone to tinker with your mind, which is the doorway to the inner man or spirit.

For hypnosis to be effective, the individual must allow himself to go into a passive mind state so that he can be manipulated by the hypnotist in whatever direction they may have agreed upon beforehand.

A passive mind state is dangerous because the mind is left unguarded and consequently susceptible to any spirit that may be waiting for just such an opportunity. This is not to say that every case of hypnosis results in demon possession, but it can be the beginning of a very negative experience that can affect the person spiritually.

I remember the case of a doctor friend of mine. She received the baptism of the Holy Spirit but had never experienced freedom of expression in her prayer language. I noticed that whenever the subject of hypnosis came up in our conversation, she was immediately defensive. One day I asked if she had ever used it in her practice.

"Not really," she answered, "I just put my patients in a very light trance to help reduce the pain."

In my studies I found that the trance that relieves pain in the patient is actually the deepest kind of all. When I informed her of this, she smiled sheepishly. I quickly told her that if she wanted to play games she could do it by herself.

At this, she acknowledged that I was correct and prayed with me, renouncing the practice. Immediately, she had a fluency in her prayer language that she had never enjoyed previously.

We must never allow anyone to tinker with our minds, which are the doorways to the inner man or spirit. Neither should we clear our minds or set them up like miniature screens for thoughts to be emblazoned across it. Nor should we chant special words over and over again to attain a certain state of mind. Satan has access to our minds as he tries to interject his thoughts and will upon us. When we leave them blank, for whatever or whoever to put something into it, we are just asking for trouble.

Subliminal messages are being recorded into music and other relaxing sounds to convey messages to the mind. More and more people are being harassed mentally and emotionally after listening to worldly motivational tapes and New Age music. These can be devilish devices used to neutralize unsuspecting persons.

God's Way of Speaking to Us

God's method of dealing with us is always through our hearts or spirits. Obviously, it is apparent who will be left to fill your mind if it is left unguarded.

Meditation on God's Word is not an exercise of the mind, but of the spirit that refreshes us in a spiritual way.

If you have been a hypnotist or been hypnotized, it is necessary to ask forgiveness for that sin, bind the spirit of divination in the name of Jesus, and promise God you will never do it again.

One person related to me that she could see herself enter into an elevator that went down to different levels and doors opening in her mind as she was being hypnotized. She had to reverse the process and shut all the doors in the name of Jesus before she could get any spiritual liberty.

Paul revealed that the successful follower of Christ renews his mind by immersing it in the Word of God to keep from being forced into the world's mold and also to find the good, acceptable, and perfect will of God. *"And be not conformed to this world: but be ye transformed by the renewing of your mind, that ye may prove what is that good, and acceptable, and perfect, will of God"* (Romans 12:2).

Magic—Sorcery

"Magic is universal, and may be 'black' or 'white.' Black magic attempts to produce evil results through such methods as curses, spells, destruction of models of one's enemy, and alliance with evil spirits. It often takes the form of witchcraft. White magic tries to undo curses or spells, and to use occult forces for the good of oneself and others. The magician tries to compel a god, demon, or spirit to work for him; or he follows a pattern of occult practices to bend psychic forces to his will."[3]

In today's language, a magician or sorcerer would be called a witch.

Notes

Meditation on God's Word refreshes our spirits.

NOTES

Included in the list of those who will be cast in the lake of fire are sorcerers. *"But the fearful, and unbelieving, and the abominable, and murderers, and whoremongers, and sorcerers, and idolaters, and all liars, shall have their part in the lake which burneth with fire and brimstone: which is the second death"* (Revelation 21:8).

Paul listed *"witchcraft"* as one of the *"works of the flesh"* in Galatians 5:19–20. He went on to say in verse 21 that *"they which do such things shall not inherit the kingdom of God."*

Observe the progression downward. First, the process begins in the fleshly desires. Whether it is a quest for special powers or attention, the person begins entertaining a fascination for such things on a fleshly level. As the desire leads to actions, the deadly roots begin entwining themselves around the will of the individual, allowing the strongman to enter the picture as he becomes more and more of a dominant force.

This is of course the usual pattern Satan uses for all sin. The best way to keep from falling into temptation is to resist and cut it off when the first fascination begins.

John Newport states in his book *Demons, Demons, Demons* that there are five thousand witches in New York, ten thousand in Los Angeles, and in the entire United States there are one half as many witches as clergymen.[4] In view of the explosion of the occult since that time, we are probably approaching the day when witches will outnumber clergymen.

It is imperative that God's people learn how to do battle on a personal basis with the demonic forces operating not only in the jungles of Africa but right here in our nation. Only then will we be able to force back the hordes of evil long enough to reach this world with the gospel, which is God's number one priority at this time.

PROGNOSTICATION

What concerns me is the believers who cross the line into demonic areas because of ignorance. Handwriting analysis is a good example of this. It is merely a modern variation of what the Bible refers to as "prognostication," in which handwriting becomes the prop instead of bones, tea leaves, tarot cards, bumps on the head, lines on the palm, etc. The end results, however, are the same. By the study of handwriting they seek to prognosticate, or tell an individual's personal characteristics, and, as a result, their probable future.

Handwriting Analysis

A few years ago, it came to my attention that an assistant pastor's wife was heavily involved in handwriting analysis. She had been analyzing not only the pastor's handwriting samples but also those of the people in the church, many of them without their knowledge. She felt this would help her husband deal with them.

When I pointed out the dangers inherent in such a practice, she became angry. I indicated in the Word what God had to say about prognostication and told her that if she continued now, after being warned, she could no longer claim ignorance. From that point on she and her family would be out of the protecting hand of God.

She stormed away, informing me that her mother, who was supposedly a good Christian, had taught her how to do it and therefore it could not be bad.

A few days later, she was driving down the road when the motor in her car suddenly caught fire. She barely had time to pull off the road and scramble to safety before the car exploded in flames. Instead of serving as confirmation of what I had told her, it enraged her all the more and she accused me of putting some kind of hex on her. She later had an affair with a married man she ensnared in her web of deceit.

Church Magic

Another seemingly innocent practice is the use of magic in churches to entertain the children and youth. It may be true that a few magic tricks seem harmless enough. But when it is traced back to its root, magic and sorcery are basically one and the same.

"The Exodus record says that the Egyptian magicians copied Moses in turning the rods into serpents (7:11),

Notes

NOTES

in turning the water into blood (7:12), and in producing frogs (8:7), but failed to produce the lice (8:18–19) and were themselves incapacitated by the boils (9:11). The account leaves us free to decide whether they were clever conjurors or whether they used occult methods."[5]

Children have a difficult time differentiating between church and occult magic. They naturally assume that all magic is OK. After all, they reason, isn't it pretty much the same as what we see in children's church?

It seems to me that we can find something better to do with the precious time we have to teach God's Word to our children than dabbling with something that has satanic roots.

WATER WITCHING

The very name *water witching* should give a clue as to which domain it falls under. Divining for water is another way of putting it. When you really stop to think about it, there is no natural law that would cause a stick, held a certain way in someone's hands, to be drawn downward to a source of water deep in the ground.

Hosea instructed the Israelites that they were not to ask counsel of *"their stocks, and their staff"* but of God (Hosea 4:12). They had begun to worship their divining rods and staffs and, as a result, God labeled it an abomination to Him.

If God could provide water for the Israelites in the desert for forty years, couldn't He also show where water is located today if we ask Him to guide us? He has given us nine gifts of the Spirit, and among them is a word of knowledge to show us the things we need to know.

SOUVENIRS AND IDOLS

As missionaries, we have lived in foreign countries where idols and relics are occasionally brought home by people for souvenirs. To our horror, we learned that some factories allow the priests and witch doctors to pronounce their incantations over the items before they are taken to market for sale. And of course many of the idols have been dug up from graves and represent evil spirits.

I recommend that you do as I did. Go through your house with a fine-tooth comb and destroy anything that even appears like the occult or has anything to do with foreign religions. Look very carefully. You may be surprised at what you find. Even if it is expensive, break it to bits in the name of Jesus. Under no circumstances should you sell it so that someone else gets hit with the curse.

Let me insert a word of caution here. Clean your own house. Leave your neighbors' and your friends' houses for them to clean. God can speak to them just as He speaks to you.

The command of God is very explicit.

> *The graven images of their gods shall ye burn with fire: thou shalt not desire the silver or gold that is on them, nor take it unto thee, lest thou be snared therein: for it is an abomination to the* Lord *thy God.* ***Neither shalt thou bring an abomination into thine house, lest thou be a cursed thing like it****: but thou shalt utterly detest it, and thou shalt utterly abhor it; for it is a cursed thing.* (Deuteronomy 7:25–26, emphasis added)

Ouija Boards

Ouija boards are not cute playthings. They can be utilized by demons to draw people into a satanic web as dangerous as what a spider uses to trap flies.

A friend of mine, her husband, and another couple decided to experiment with an Ouija board one evening. They asked the power behind the board, "Who are you?"

"You know who I am," was the answer.

They asked the same question a second time and received the same answer again.

Persistently they inquired the third time, "Who are you?"

The game ended abruptly with the shocking reply, "Go to hell!"

Next they tried levitation. The two couples were able to raise a table by placing their hands flat on the top. But one night the table rose into the air and began dancing

Notes

NOTES

so violently they couldn't stop it. Frightened, they left the house for a few hours until things calmed down and returned to normal.

These things are not something to mess around with unless you are ready to accept the long-term consequences—life on Satan's terms.

GAMES

Make sure you know what kind of table games and even video games your children are playing. Many of them have occult formats, teachings, and symbolisms. They are now teaching young people how to cast spells and contact spirit guides through these so-called games. Just because it is fun doesn't mean it is wholesome.

CARTOONS AND TOYS

Beware of the occult teaching that is being written into cartoons for younger children. They are being programmed with Eastern mysticism and witchcraft practices. Take time to find out which ones are taboo for your child.

Many of today's cartoons have dolls on the market to represent their main cast of characters. Some of these are demonic in looks and others are not. They invoke the imaginations of the children to live in the occult and even welcome the displacement of God as the real Master of our universe.

REBELLION—STUBBORNNESS

Before I pray with you, let me read a Scripture that is really a study by itself but which does pertain to what we have been discussing in this chapter. *"For rebellion is as the sin of witchcraft, and stubbornness is as iniquity and idolatry"* (1 Samuel 15:23).

The basic sin of witchcraft is rebellion against the commandments of God. Instead of choosing God's way, these people accepted an inferior god, Satan, and stubbornly refused to give God His rightful place in their lives. If you rebelliously go about doing your own thing without submitting to authority or consulting God, it is as odious to

God as if you were drinking blood in a witch's coven. God demands to be number one in our lives.

If you haven't accepted Christ as your Savior, simply say, "Lord Jesus Christ, forgive me of my sins and accept me as Your child. I accept You as my personal Savior and promise to follow the instruction of Your Word from this day on. Thank You, Jesus, for saving me from all my sins. Amen."

Now that you are a child of God, according to Matthew 18:18, we are going to bind the strongman, the spirit of divination, and loose the power of the Holy Spirit in your life.

"Father, I come to You in the name of Jesus, thanking You for Your Word and the Holy Spirit that has made me aware of my sin. Forgive me of any past or current involvement in occult activities. I love You, God, and I want to live a life that is pleasing to You.

"Satan, in the name of Jesus, I bind you and the spirit of divination according to Matthew 18:18, which clearly states, *"Whatsoever ye shall bind on earth shall be bound in heaven."* Consider any pact that was made either by me or my family in the past to be broken once and for all. You have no hold on my life or that of my family from now on in the name of Jesus.

"Thank You, Lord Jesus, for freeing me, and I worship You. According to Matthew 18:18, which promises, *"Whatsoever ye shall bind on earth shall be bound in heaven,"* I loose the power of the Holy Spirit in my life to restore and fill me with Your power. Give me a thirst for Your Word. Thank You, Lord, for hearing and answering my prayer. Amen."

NOTES

Familiar Spirit

Leviticus 19:31

Necromancer

Deuteronomy 18:11; 1 Chronicles 10:13

Medium

1 Samuel 28

Peeping & Muttering

Isaiah 8:19; 29:4; 59:3

Passive Mind States, Dreamers

Jeremiah 23:16, 25, 32; 27:9–10

Drugs (Greek, pharmakos)

Galatians 5:20; Revelation 9:21; 18:23; 21:8; 22:15

Spiritist

1 Samuel 28

Clairvoyant

1 Samuel 28:7–8

Yoga

Jeremiah 29:8

False Prophecy

Isaiah 8:19; 29:4

Roots are
"...works of the flesh."
—Galatians 5:19–21

"By their fruits ye shall know them."
—Matthew 7:20

According to Matthew 18:18...

Bind: Familiar Spirit

Loose: Holy Spirit and Gifts

1 Corinthians 12:9–12

CHAPTER 2

Familiar Spirit

A familiar spirit and a spirit of divination are very similar in nature. In fact, it is not unusual for a number of strongmen to gang up together if it serves their purpose.

When there is no clear-cut distinction between these two spirits, I just bind both of them at the same time in the name of Jesus.

A familiar spirit is usually involved in the areas of necromancy (supposed consultation with the dead), spirit mediums, clairvoyance, yoga, spiritists, psychic powers and prophecy, transcendental meditation (T.M.), extra-sensory perception (ESP), cocaine, crack, and other mind-altering drugs, internal trance inspiration or direct second sight such as dreams, internal visions, and passive mind states, as well as trance channeling.

The ability to contact spirits is often passed from one generation to the next within receptive families, which may account in part for its name, "familiar." The word *familiar* comes from the root word *family*.

Even though someone may have accepted Christ as his Savior, it is still necessary to renounce in an audible voice any past experiences he, or members of his family, may have had with any of these practices. It is possible for a Christian to be harassed by demonic forces that believe they still have access rights to him because of their past affiliations with either him or his family.

Most of us are unaware of the relationships our grandparents or great-grandparents may have had with Satan. We don't know whether they delved into the occult and other forbidden practices, either purposely or through ignorance. Understand now, our relatives' pasts cannot make us demon possessed if we are now living according to God's Word. It simply means that we must close those doors permanently in our lives, which we would certainly have done

NOTES

NOTES

"Threads" from the old life often must be cut before we find liberty.

earlier had we known it was necessary. We inform Satan and his harassing demons that, based on the Word of God, we are breaking all pacts we or our relatives may have made in the past with him because we are now under new ownership. We are new creatures in Christ Jesus.

In our personal ministry, we have found that these "threads" from the old life have to be severed before people can find full liberty in the Spirit. We automatically lead people in a prayer of renunciation from occultic, psychic practices in our crusades, especially when they want to receive the baptism of the Holy Spirit. It certainly doesn't harm them to do so, and we have seen the freedom it brings to those who want the fullness of the Spirit in their lives.

God's Word is very explicit where a familiar spirit is involved. *"A man also or woman that hath a familiar spirit, or that is a wizard, shall surely be put to death: they shall stone them with stones: their blood shall be upon them"* (Leviticus 20:27).

God is so vehement in His denunciation of these practices because people who seek unholy spirits for guidance are actually breaking the first commandment. This type of spirit communication brings judgment on the participant according to Exodus 20:5, *"For I the LORD thy God am a jealous God, visiting the iniquity of the fathers upon the children unto the third and fourth generation of them that hate me."*

SAUL

The sad case of Saul and the witch of Endor illustrates the futility and tragedy that occurred after God's prophet, Samuel, was dead.

> *And when Saul saw the host of the Philistines, he was afraid, and his heart greatly trembled. And when Saul inquired of the LORD, the LORD answered him not, neither by dreams, nor by Urim, nor by prophets. Then said Saul unto his servants, Seek me a woman that hath a familiar spirit, that I may go to her, and inquire of her. And his servants said to him, Behold, there is a woman that hath a familiar spirit at Endor. And*

Saul disguised himself, and put on other raiment, and he went, and two men with him, and they came to the woman by night: and he said, I pray thee, divine unto me by the familiar spirit, and bring me him up, whom I shall name unto thee. And the woman said unto him, Behold, thou knowest what Saul hath done, how he hath cut off those that have familiar spirits, and the wizards, out of the land: wherefore then layest thou a snare for my life, to cause me to die? And Saul sware to her by the Lord*, saying, As the* Lord *liveth, there shall no punishment happen to thee for this thing. Then said the woman, Whom shall I bring up unto thee? And he said, Bring me up Samuel. And when the woman saw Samuel, she cried with a loud voice: and the woman spake to Saul, saying, Why hast thou deceived me? for thou art Saul. And the king said unto her, Be not afraid: for what sawest thou? And the woman said unto Saul, I saw gods ascending out of the earth. And he said unto her, What form is he of? And she said, An old man cometh up; and he is covered with a mantle. And Saul perceived that it was Samuel, and he stooped with his face to the ground, and bowed himself. And Samuel said to Saul, Why hast thou disquieted me, to bring me up? And Saul answered, I am sore distressed; for the Philistines make war against me, and God is departed from me, and answereth me no more, neither by prophets, nor by dreams: therefore I have called thee, that thou mayest make known unto me what I shall do. Then said Samuel, Wherefore then dost thou ask of me, seeing the* Lord *is departed from thee, and is become thine enemy? And the* Lord *hath done to him, as he spake by me: for the* Lord *hath rent the kingdom out of thine hand, and given it to thy neighbour, even to David: because thou obeyedst not the voice of the* Lord*, nor executedst his fierce wrath upon Amalek, therefore hath the* Lord *done this thing unto thee this day. Moreover the* Lord *will also deliver Israel with thee into the hand of the Philistines: and to morrow shalt thou and thy sons be with me: the* Lord *also shall deliver the host of Israel into the hand of the Philistines.*

(1 Samuel 28:5–19)

Notes

NOTES

What Really Happened?

There are a number of clues here that indicate what actually took place that night. Verses 7 and 8 clearly state that Saul wanted information from a familiar spirit because he wasn't on speaking terms with God. (See verse 6.) If God refused to answer Saul through regular channels, He certainly would not use a witch with a familiar spirit operating through her. Always remember, when God wants to speak to His people, He uses either the Holy Spirit or the written Word of God. God will *never* use an unclean spirit to communicate with mankind.

The only conclusion we can draw from this is that a familiar spirit or demon impersonated Samuel. Demons are familiar with what is going on in the world, and they use such information to predict, sidetrack, instill fear, or confuse humanity.

The sad fact is that Saul received exactly what he asked for: demonic guidance that led him down the path to suicide and eternal separation from God. *"Saul died for his transgression…for asking counsel of one that had a familiar spirit, to inquire of it; and inquired not of the LORD: therefore he slew him"* (1 Chronicles 10:13–14). If there was ever an illustration of how far astray the pseudoguidance of mediums and necromancers can lead an individual, it is Saul.

Mind Readers

Possibly you have seen people on television who appeared to read the minds of complete strangers. The truth is that, unless they were con artists, with an accomplice feeding them information via special code words, they were probably tuned in to a familiar spirit.

False Prophets

The prophetic information dispensed these days by so-called prophets ranges from the prediction of the deaths of leading world figures to a cure for cancer. Considering the condition of today's world, you would think people would prefer *not* to know what is going to happen. But frightened people seem to prefer even the worst prediction to nagging uncertainty.

Although there is much fakery in this business, many of the predictions do come true. Satan has some knowledge, especially in the areas of disaster and death. He ought to, since he is the cause of such things, according to John 10:10.

I observed Jean Dixon predict the New York blackout down to the smallest detail some years ago on television one year before it happened.

Mrs. Dixon is probably one of the most popular seers on the scene today. Many newspapers and magazines traditionally feature her predictions for the year on the first of January.

A prophecy that she classes as her most important, and indeed the reason why she has been given prophetic ability, concerns a "child born in the Middle East on February 5, 1962." She claims he "will revolutionize the world and eventually unite all warring creeds and sects into one all-embracing faith."[1]

She also believes that an experience she had with a snake is a sign that "we must look to the east for growth and to the west for the ending of things." The snake wrapped itself around her body and she could see "the all-knowing wisdom of the ages" in its eyes.[2]

Even though she gives God the glory for her prophetic ability, we can only conclude that she is being used by a familiar spirit that deludes those who listen to her. God does not use snakes to convey His plans for the future.

God's Guidance

God's method of directing the lives of His children is found in His divinely inspired Word. The psalmist told us God's Word *"is a lamp unto my feet, and a light unto my path"* (Psalm 119:105).

When we read and meditate upon the Bible, the Holy Spirit teaches us the truths we need to live successful, righteous lives. Jesus instructed the disciples to depend on the Holy Spirit for future guidance. *"But the Comforter, which is the Holy Ghost, whom the Father will send in my name, he shall teach you all things, and bring all things to your remembrance, whatsoever I have said unto you"* (John 14:26).

Notes

God directs His children's lives through His Word.

NOTES

CLAIRVOYANTS

Finally, there are psychics who claim to be clairvoyant. Energized by a familiar spirit, they see objects or people who may have been lost. Police departments sometimes contact these people to locate lost children or clues to a murder case or even the body of the victim. Who would be more knowledgeable about where the murder victim was located than demons who probably inspired the killer to commit the crime in the first place?

These psychics sensitize themselves to hear familiar spirits who become their "spirit guides." The guide passes on information he feels will attract and fascinate the general public. Everyone wants to get inside information so they can be one step ahead of the next person. In this way, the trap is sprung on the unsuspecting victim.

True information is given at first to gain their confidence, but eventually lies outweigh truths and the unsuspecting dupe is entangled. He is then led deeper and deeper into the "new truths and revelations." The rest of the world is considered to be backward compared to the knowledge he now possesses. Without God's Word for guidance, the familiar spirit feeds him the most outrageous nonsense, and he believes it is a sacred prophecy from a distant planet, or even a message from God Himself.

EDGAR CAYCE

The late Edgar Cayce was such a case in point. He would go into a trance, and the familiar spirit would take over, giving out medical information to cure people of various ailments and diseases. Because these "readings," as they are called, seemed to work, the followers believed they were from God. But it didn't end there. The spirit guide continued leading them on into reincarnation and other false beliefs. "Reincarnation, then, is not a theory; it is a practical code of ethics directly affecting human mortality. Edgar Cayce's readings accept it unequivocally...."[3]

"The results [of the thousands of Cayce's readings] are being released as they are secured through the association publications, and the members, whose numbers continue to increase, are the recipients weekly and monthly of the essence of everything that issued from the subconscious of Edgar Cayce...."[4]

The Bible ceases to be the primary source of knowledge to these followers of Cayce because they have information that they believe updates God's Word.

Cayce himself said, "All my life I've wondered what it is that comes through me. It could be of the devil; it could be of God; it could be just foolishness.

"If it were the devil it would produce evil. To my knowledge it never has produced evil."[5]

But he was mistaken: it is evil to lead people away from the truth of God's Word.

Transcendental Meditation

In transcendental meditation, the repetition of a special word used to attain relaxation and other assorted benefits. Many times the individual doesn't realize that his special word is the name of a demon, which he is actually calling to come and guide or possess him.

How amazing that religions from India and the Far East are catching on in the United States. Our supposedly Christian country is turning to heathenism in those cases where God's Word has been rejected as the only road to peace of mind.

The students of TM receive an alleviation of some symptoms when they begin their meditation. The devil is astute. He makes sure the hook is deeply implanted before he begins his insidious process of bondage. Relaxation may be achieved, but it doesn't stop there. Just look at India with its hunger and devastation, and you will have a grim picture of the final stages of these demonic practices. If these religions are so wonderful, why haven't they helped the people of India, who have been practicing them for centuries? The only benefits it has brought them is hunger, starvation, and havoc because that is the devil's contribution to the human race.

I met a lady in one of our Costa Rican crusades whose two children were experiencing problems with their

Notes

NOTES

speech and vocal chords. The Holy Spirit impressed me that the woman had visited a witch. When I questioned her about it, she denied that she had.

"Oh yes, you have been to a witch within the past three years," I insisted. "Now tell me the truth, when did you take your children to a witch?"

She broke down and confessed that it was true. Her children had been suffering from a minor ailment, and the witch had apparently healed them. But then the more serious problem had begun manifesting itself, and now she was frightened. When she confessed her sin and renounced her participation with the occult, Jesus healed her children.

Satan appears to help the victim, initially, only to wrap him in bondage many times worse than before until he is hopelessly entangled in his lies, sicknesses, and practices of darkness.

ESP

We have all heard of practitioners of extrasensory perception who bend spoons and metal, start broken watches, and transport objects from one place to another seemingly by their powers of mental concentration.

In reality, they are in league with demons, who use these antics to attract people's attention. The public is encouraged to do these mental feats themselves. They are told to experiment with their exceptional mental powers. The sad fact is that the demons can take advantage of these occasions to lead the mind-control candidate into deeper occult pitfalls.

Peeping and Muttering

A subtle form of false prophecy that seeks to infiltrate prayer groups, and even Christian churches, uses a form of "speaking in tongues" that seems valid to Christians who are not grounded in the Word of God. Actually these "tongues" sound more like insects clicking and chirping away.

I observed such an exhibition one day by one of the leaders of a lady's prayer group. She would "pray" in a rapid, monotone, under-the-breath type of "kla, kla, kla, chuka, chuka, chuka, chuka" sound. Then she would surface with a vision that she had seen displayed on the screen of her mind.

As I listened to her, I felt a revulsion in my spirit that was difficult to suppress. She included me in some of her so-called prophecies, and my spirit did not bear witness that it was from God. The prophecies did not come true, but in the meantime other innocent but ignorant ladies started using this particular brand of "prayer language."

God showed me after a time of prayer and study in His Word that we were dealing with a satanic influence. Here is what I found, *"And when they shall say unto you, Seek unto them that have familiar spirits, and unto wizards that* ***peep****, and that* ***mutter****: should not a people seek unto their God? for the living to the dead?"* (Isaiah 8:19, emphasis added).

God Speaks to Our Spirits

One of the tip-offs to the origin of the visions was the fact that they were shown on the "screen" of her mind. God's way of communicating with us is through our spirits, not our minds. *"God is a Spirit: and they that worship him must worship him in spirit and in truth"* (John 4:24).

Beware of anything that originates with or magnifies the human mind. That is Satan's playground unless it is renewed each day by the Word. God's gifts of the Spirit are pure and uplifting. Don't be afraid to point out the errors of those who stray from God's methods of operation by showing what the Word has to say about it. In the case mentioned above, I gave the ladies a Bible study exposing the error for what it was, a trick of the devil. The leader involved was furious with me, which was a clear indicator of her spiritual condition. The ladies who had been duped soon dropped that foolishness and thanked me for helping them see how God's gifts of the Spirit operate.

If we are truly walking with God, I have found that we also will manifest a humble, teachable spirit.

Notes

God's gifts of the Spirit are pure and uplifting.

NOTES

Psychic Phenomena—Poltergeist Activity

Psychic phenomena and poltergeists can both fascinate and terrorize families living in haunted houses. Pianos play as the keys are pressed by invisible hands, cabinets rattle, dishes fall, footsteps are heard where no one is visible, ghosts materialize and disappear, frigid air is felt in unexplainable places, and chains are heard to rattle where no chains exist. All of these manifestations are nothing but demons tantalizing and taunting the poor people involved.

Some believe they are the spirits of people who died violent deaths and are still disturbed as they wander around the site of their demise. But God's Word states emphatically that people do not wander around after death. They go either to Hades or heaven, according to whether they have rejected or accepted Christ as their Savior. *"And as it is appointed unto men once to die, but after this the judgment"* (Hebrews 9:27).

If we come into contact with such demonic activity, we need only rattle the demons back into their cages where they belong in the name of Jesus. There is no need to put up with such nonsense. Demons love to put on a sideshow if they can get an audience to watch.

"For God is not the author of confusion, but of peace, as in all churches of the saints" (1 Corinthians 14:33).

Drugs

Although addictive drugs belong under the spirit of bondage, yet Satan can use the passive mind state brought about by the hallucinogenic drugs such as LSD, cocaine, crack, alcohol, and prescription drugs like Valium and Librium to activate everything from depression to possession in those who experiment with or depend on such substances.

We cannot allow our minds to be fuzzed up. Satan will take advantage of our weakened condition while we are in that state if we are not on guard.

Remember, anyone who strays, either consciously or unconsciously, into Satan's area of operations by participating in the activities mentioned in this chapter can expect to be harassed in one way or another by the powers of evil. Demons feel they have the right to do so until such time as they are informed differently in the name of Jesus, backed up by God's Word.

Deliverance

If you are dealing with someone who wants and needs deliverance from a familiar spirit, show him that he must first accept Christ as his Savior. Point out in God's Word the seriousness of relying on Satan for guidance instead of God. Then, bind the strongman in the name of Jesus, release the power of the Holy Spirit in his life, and lead him in a prayer of renunciation of all occult and psychic practices. After he has been delivered, it is a good idea to encourage him to immediately receive the baptism of the Holy Spirit so he will have the spiritual discernment and power to resist the familiar spirit's attempts to move in again at a later date. Teach him to stand firm by using God's Word like a sword to fend off the enemy's thrusts. And lastly, show him it is extremely important to utterly refuse any temptation to return to his former life.

The best way to be free and stay clear of demonic influences is to *"be filled with the Spirit"* (Ephesians 5:18) and to *"let the word of Christ dwell in you richly in all wisdom"* (Colossians 3:16).

The insanity of seeking the things of Satan is that his power is inferior to God's. Why settle for second-best when we can have God's power and wisdom in our lives and go first-class?

If you haven't accepted Christ as your Savior, simply say in an audible voice, in all sincerity from the depths of your heart, "Lord Jesus Christ, forgive me of my sins and accept me as Your child. I accept You as my personal Savior, and I promise to follow the instructions of Your Word from this day on. Thank You, Jesus, for saving me from all my sins. Amen."

Now that you are a member of the family of God, according to Matthew 18:18 you can bind the strongman, a

Notes

NOTES

familiar spirit, and loose the power of the Holy Spirit in your life.

"Father, I come to You in the name of Jesus, thanking You for Your Word and the Holy Spirit, which has made me aware of my sin. Forgive me of any past or present involvement in the occult activities of Satan. I love You, God, and I want to live according to Your Word for the rest of my life.

"Satan, in the name of Jesus I bind you and your familiar spirit according to Matthew 18:18, which states clearly that, *'Whatsoever ye shall bind on earth shall be bound in heaven.'* You must consider any pact that I or any members of my family have made to be null and void from this point on.

"Thank You, Lord Jesus, for freeing me. I praise Your holy name. According to Matthew 18:18, *'Whatsoever ye shall loose on earth shall be loosed in heaven,'* I loose the power of the Holy Spirit in my life to restore and fill me with Your power. Give me a deep desire to read Your Word. Thank You, Jesus, for hearing and answering my prayer. I promise to follow Your Word the rest of my life."

Notes

Spirit of Jealousy

Numbers 5:14

Murder
Genesis 4:8

Revenge, Spite
Proverbs 6:34; 14:16–17

Jealousy
Numbers 5:14, 30

Anger, Rage
Genesis 4:5–6; Proverbs 6:34; 14:29; 22:24–25; 29:22–23

Hatred
Genesis 37:3, 4, 8; 1 Thessalonians 4:8

Strife
Proverbs 10:12

Cruelty
Song of Solomon 8:6; Proverbs 27:4

Extreme Competition
Genesis 4:4–5

Contention
Proverbs 13:10

Cause Divisions
Galatians 5:19

Envy
Proverbs 14:30

Roots are
"...works of the flesh."
—Galatians 5:19–21

"By their fruits ye shall know them."
—Matthew 7:20

According to Matthew 18:18...

Bind: Spirit of Jealousy

Loose: Love of God

1 Corinthians 13; Ephesians 5:2

Chapter 3

Spirit of Jealousy

Jealousy, along with pride, is probably the oldest sin in the universe. They existed even before our earth, as we know it now, was created.

Lucifer was perfect, beautiful, and occupied the highest standing among God's created beings; but he became jealous of God. Jealousy is mentioned by name in Numbers 5:14. *"How art thou fallen from heaven, O Lucifer, son of the morning!...For thou hast said in thine heart, I will ascend into heaven, I will exalt my throne above the stars of God...I will be like the most High"* (Isaiah 14:12–14; see also Ezekiel 28:12–19). Because of his rebellion, Lucifer was reduced to being Satan, the ruler of darkness, and thrown out of heaven.

Later, God recreated our present world and placed Adam and Eve in the garden of Eden. He longed to have fellowship on a daily basis with the world's first couple. A beautiful atmosphere of love and unity pervaded the garden until Satan entered the picture.

Adam and Eve sinned, breaking the cord of fellowship with God, and soon they had to adjust to a different environment outside the garden. Life became a difficult battle against the elements, pain, thorns, and thistles.

Satan regained dominion of the earth through the fall of man. He will continue to exercise this right through those members of the human race who cooperate with him until he is cast into the bottomless pit at the end of the great tribulation. After he is released for a season at the close of the millennium, he will be cast into his final destination, the lake of fire. (See Revelation 20:1.)

Murder

The Bible says that Cain was *"very wroth* [angry], *and his countenance fell"* (Genesis 4:5). People who will not

Notes

NOTES

control their anger open themselves up to the strongman of jealousy.

Our prisons are full of murderers, wife beaters, and child abusers who allowed rage to push them beyond the normal limits. "I don't know why I did it" is a common phrase heard by law enforcement officers.

JOSEPH

The story of Joseph is a further example of how the spirit of jealousy does its insidious work.

> *Now Israel loved Joseph more than all his children, because he was the son of his old age: and he made him a coat of many colours. And when his brethren saw that their father loved him more than all his brethren, they hated him, and could not speak peaceably unto him.... And his brethren said to him, Shalt thou indeed reign over us? or shalt thou indeed have dominion over us? And they hated him yet the more for his dreams, and for his words.* (Genesis 37:3–4, 8)

Joseph was wearing a coat of many colors, which marked him by the traditions of that day as the chief heir of the family. His ten elder brothers could see the significance of this, and it triggered jealous, hateful, murderous thoughts. They refused to be pushed aside so easily by their doting father as the rightful heads of the tribe. So they got rid of Joseph by selling him to the first camel caravan that passed by.

REVENGE

Revenge is another manifestation of the spirit of jealousy. It is true that Israel had no right to favor Joseph over his other sons. But that did not give the brothers any right to brutalize Joseph. The damning factor in the whole tragedy was that Joseph's brothers enjoyed every minute of it. But they eventually discovered that *"vengeance is mine; I will repay, saith the Lord"* (Romans 12:19).

When God squared the accounts, they were truly settled. Joseph did not have to raise a finger against his brothers. He *did* have to wait a few years, but God's people must always have the faith and confidence necessary to allow God to sort things out according to His wisdom and timing.

The brothers paid for their hatred and revenge more dearly than they could have ever dreamed. Although they convinced Jacob that Joseph was dead, they probably heard their father mourning Joseph's memory day and night. They just *thought* they had gotten rid of Joseph. But then jealousy, hatred, and revenge never accomplish what they lead us to believe they will do.

In the end, the brothers were brought right back around to their original problem and made to admit that they had been terribly mistaken.

Note that, although Joseph didn't let his brothers off easy when they came to Egypt looking for food, his broken spirit does indicate that his motivation was not one of revenge. He was merely a tool in God's hand to ensure that his ten brothers would never forget the lesson they had to learn.

> *Dearly beloved, avenge not yourselves, but rather give place unto wrath* [Give room for the civil laws to be enforced and officers to do their duty[1]]: *for it is written, Vengeance is mine; I will repay, saith the Lord. Therefore if thine enemy hunger, feed him; if he thirst, give him drink: for in so doing thou shalt heap coals of fire on his head. Be not overcome of evil, but overcome evil with good.* (Romans 12:19–21)

This is the beauty of doing it God's way. Instead of carrying around a load of resentment, jealousy, and hatred, we are able to just turn the whole thing over to God and observe how He takes care of it.

Personally, when I have followed this godly law, I have seen some interesting things happen. People who have taken advantage of me, doing hurtful, spiteful things because of envy or jealousy, have been brought to their knees by the hand of God and forced to admit their wrongdoing. This not only exonerated me, but I was freed to resume a friendship that the strongman had tried to destroy. That is overcoming evil with good!

NOTES

If we turn our resentment, jealousy, and hatred over to God, He will take care of it.

NOTES

COMPETITION

A symptom of the spirit of jealousy that is largely overlooked in this day of fierce competition, both on the sports field and in business, is an attitude of *unnatural* competition.

It is true that we should be goal oriented and strive to do an excellent job in whatever we are asked to do. The problem is when the drive to supersede drives us in *unnatural* ways.

In the case of both Cain and Abel and Joseph and his ten brothers, this competitive spirit got out of hand. The same attitude is evident among football players today who try to injure an opposing player so their team will win. The saying, "Winning is not important...it's everything," is the favorite phrase of these overachievers who are in danger of getting more carried away than they realize.

I remember a basketball game back in high school when our team had fallen behind early in the game. As the contest came down to the closing minutes, one of our players, playing like he was possessed, led our team to an incredible comeback, closing the gap to just a few points. But it was to no avail. The seconds ticked off the clock and, just before the buzzer sounded, ending the game, our most valuable player took out his overwhelming frustration on the opposing star player by knocking him cold with a right to the jaw. The crowd was stunned into silence by the unprovoked viciousness of the attack.

The officials quickly led the attacker away so he could calm down. They later attributed the whole incident to a case of the player being so intent on winning he temporarily lost control of himself and was therefore not completely responsible for his actions.

How sad to see fathers and mothers trying to instill this competitive spirit into their Little Leaguers so they will scratch and claw their way to victory, using whatever tactics it takes to win, win, win.

An interview with actor James Caan gave a glimpse into this world of competition when it revealed that "he's always been driven by the desire to be a winner. 'My need for competition is so fierce it turns off my friends,' he said.

'They can't understand why I never let up...why I can't play a friendly game of basketball, tennis, or any sport.'

"'Well, I just can't. If I play at all, I play to win. My determination frightens any man. Peter Falk says of me, 'The guy's crazy. You have to tell him to let up...that it ain't the Olympics.'"[2]

Just think how this competitive spirit could spill over into other areas of life, and with what tragic consequences. Can you imagine being married to a person, no matter how attractive, who never wants to lose a game or an argument?

Seedbeds

How does the spirit of jealousy gain entrance into our lives? Here are some works of the flesh that can spring up into full-blown problems: covetousness, envying, debate, strife, hatred, divisions, jealousy, and resentments. These are deadly seedlings that begin growing in our lives when we are not careful. If they are not pulled up, including the roots, they grow bigger and bigger, dominating the individual to a greater degree every day. As Satan observes this softness to sin, he directs specific strongmen to take advantage of that weakness until such bondage exists in the individual that he needs supernatural help to be set free.

When we notice these symptoms working in our lives, it is imperative to take action in the name of Jesus against them before they gain greater control.

The love of God is the only effective deterrent against jealousy and the other works related to it. *"Hatred stirreth up strifes: but love covereth all sins"* (Proverbs 10:12).

"And walk in love, as Christ also hath loved us, and hath given himself for us an offering and a sacrifice to God for a sweetsmelling savour" (Ephesians 5:2).

Once we have recognized the spiritual problem, we bind it in the name of Jesus and loose the love of Christ in its place. Then we live in continual resistance to its attempts to return. Recognize that the strongman will *always* try to come back until you prove to him by your Bible-based resistance that you have rejected once and for all that particular kind of lifestyle.

Notes

The love of God is the only deterrent to jealousy.

NOTES

Start by asking for God's forgiveness. "Father, I come to You in the name of Jesus. I recognize that I've been leaving myself open to the attacks of the spirit of jealousy. Forgive me and help me to live a life that is pleasing to You.

"Satan, in the name of Jesus I bind your spirit of jealousy according to Matthew 18:18, which tells me, *'Whatsoever ye shall bind on earth shall be bound in heaven.'* You no longer have an open door in my life through this spirit.

"Thank You, Lord, for giving me freedom over the power of the devil. According to Matthew 18:18, which promises, *'Whatsoever ye shall loose on earth shall be loosed in heaven.'* I loose the love of God in my life to flood my being so completely that I will *'overcome evil with good'* (Romans 12:21). Help me to read Your Word faithfully each day. Thank You, Lord, for hearing and answering my prayer. Amen."

Notes

Lying Spirit
2 Chronicles 18:22

Strong Deception
2 Thessalonians 2:9–13

Flattery
Psalm 78:36; Proverbs 20:19; 26:28; 29:5

Religious Bondages
Galatians 5:1

Superstitions
1 Timothy 4:7

False Prophecy
Jeremiah 23:16–17; 27:9–10; Matthew 7:15

Accusations
Revelation 12:10; Psalm 31:18

Lies
2 Chronicles 18:22; Proverbs 6:16–19

Gossip
1 Timothy 6:20; 2 Timothy 2:16

Slander
Proverbs 10:18

False Teachers
2 Peter 1–3

Roots are
"...works of the flesh."
—Galatians 5:19–21

"By their fruits ye shall know them."
—Matthew 7:20

According to Matthew 18:18...
Bind: Lying Spirit
Loose: Spirit of Truth (Jesus)
John 14:17; 15:26; 16:13

Chapter 4

Lying Spirit

It is extremely important to understand that God never changes. He is the same as He has always been. *"Jesus Christ the same yesterday, and to day, and for ever"* (Hebrews 13:8).

The balance of evidence in the Scripture shows conclusively that God *always* speaks the truth. God has never uttered a lie and never will. Satan is the expert liar and, in fact, is the inventor of lies.

In 2 Chronicles 18:20–22, it appears the Lord cooperated with a lying spirit, or strongman. The reason for this apparent contradiction is that God has only *progressively* revealed Himself to mankind through the centuries. Due to a lack of a more complete knowledge of God, there were many occasions in the Old Testament when actions attributed to God were in reality the actions of the devil. We know this now because of the further revelation of the New Testament.

The ignorance of the religious leaders of Israel was apparent even in Jesus' day when they criticized the way He cast out devils. The Pharisees said, *"This fellow doth not cast out devils, but by Beelzebub the prince of the devils"* (Matthew 12:24).

Jesus answered, *"And if Satan cast out Satan, he is divided against himself; how shall then his kingdom stand?...But if I cast out devils by the Spirit of God, then the kingdom of God is come unto you"* (Matthew 12:26, 28). He went on to warn them that attributing a work of the Holy Spirit to Satan was the unpardonable sin. (See Matthew 12:31–32.)

So it is mandatory to clearly understand what God's area of operation is in the spirit world as well as the devil's.

The False Prophets

Keeping this in mind, let's look at one of the sources in God's Word that mentions a lying spirit.

Notes

NOTES

If we choose not to obey God, He will not force us.

> *Then there came out a spirit, and stood before the LORD, and said, I will entice him. And the LORD said unto him, Wherewith? And he said, I will go out, and be a lying spirit in the mouth of all his prophets. And the LORD said, Thou shalt entice him, and thou shalt also prevail: go out, and do even so. Now therefore, behold, the LORD hath put a lying spirit in the mouth of these thy prophets, and the LORD hath spoken evil against thee.* (2 Chronicles 18:20–22)

What is really being said here? Would God, who is truth, put a lying spirit in anyone's mouth? No, if He did so, He would cease to be the truth.

What happened was that the prophets of King Ahab told the king what they knew he wanted them to say instead of what God wanted them to prophesy, so God stepped back and simply allowed them to continue on in their lies.

God still deals with mankind in this manner. We are free moral agents. If we choose not to obey God, He will not force us to do so.

SATAN: FATHER OF ALL LIES

Jesus gave us the source of all lies when he informed the Pharisees,

> *Ye are of your father the devil, and the lusts of your father ye will do. He was a murderer from the beginning, and abode not in the truth, because there is no truth in him. When he speaketh a lie, he speaketh of his own: for he is a liar, and the father of it.*
> (John 8:44)

Let me emphasize that not everyone who lies is possessed by a lying spirit. But each lie can be a step down the road to such a condition. We have all known liars who could not control themselves. However, they didn't reach that condition overnight, but over a period of time.

Some of the areas in which a lying spirit is specifically involved are: old wives tales, superstitions, gossip or backbiting, false prophets and teachers, strong delusions or deceptions, and, of course, lies.

Superstitions

It is amazing that people in our modern world still believe they can be affected by black cats crossing their paths, walking under ladders, believing seven years of bad luck follow those who break a mirror, and unlucky Friday the 13th.

But God's Word gives conclusive evidence that there is no such thing as "luck," either good or bad, for the child of God who is obediently following God's will as revealed in the Bible. We receive what we need not because of good or bad luck but because God provides it, *"according to his riches in glory by Christ Jesus"* (Philippians 4:19).

David declared,

> *The steps of a good man are ordered by the LORD: and he delighteth in his way. Though he fall, he shall not be utterly cast down: for the LORD upholdeth him with his hand. I have been young, and now am old; yet have I not seen the righteous forsaken, nor his seed begging bread.* (Psalm 37:23–25)

"Be not afraid of sudden fear, neither of the desolation of the wicked, when it cometh." We do not fear the bad luck of disasters, *"for the LORD shall be thy confidence, and shall keep thy foot from being taken"* (Proverbs 3:25–26).

When a child of God believes that bad luck can haphazardly strike him at some unfortunate turn in the road, he is not only doubting God's ability to watch over him, but he is also believing the lies of the enemy.

"We know that all things work together for good to them that love God, to them who are the called according to his purpose" (Romans 8:28).

Paul advised Timothy, *"But refuse profane and old wives' fables, and exercise thyself rather unto godliness"* (1 Timothy 4:7).

Yes, we can refuse the lies of Satan. Just don't even believe them. *"Your life is hid with Christ in God"* (Colossians 3:3). It will take more than a silly black cat walking across your path to mess up your day. In fact, if the poor cat isn't careful, *he* may be the one who suffers the bad luck if someone happens to step on his tail.

Notes

We can refuse the lies of Satan. Just don't believe them.

NOTES

GOSSIPING

Gossiping, or "backbiting" as Paul called it in Romans 1:30, is one of the most fiendish forms of lying. It hurts, ruins, and destroys innocent victims who aren't present to defend themselves.

People who would never pick up a gun and shoot someone think nothing of performing character assassination with lethal barrages of gossip.

It has been said that Christians are members of the only army in the world that kills its own wounded. In the armed forces, a soldier found aiding and abetting the enemy is court marshaled for treason and shot.

Even if the stories *are* true, we do not have the right to inform everyone else about it. Jesus said, *"Every idle word that men shall speak, they shall give account thereof in the day of judgment"* (Matthew 12:36).

What a degrading act it is for God's children to become loudspeakers for the devil's lies. How many times have we seen someone's ministry stunted, if not destroyed, by an ugly rumor that was nothing but a lie?

When the body feeds upon itself in this manner, it is actually a form of spiritual cannibalism. And who do you suppose is behind it all? You guessed it, the old granddaddy of liars, the devil. He wants to kill and maim the reputations of God's people.

Gossip isn't just a character flaw. It can possess a person to the point that, even though he hates himself for doing it, he cannot stop. He has become a compulsive gossiper, who is in the grips of a lying strongman.

Paul advised,

> *Whatsoever things are true, whatsoever things are honest, whatsoever things are just, whatsoever things are pure, whatsoever things are lovely, whatsoever things are of good report; if there be any virtue, and if there be any praise, think on these things.*
>
> (Philippians 4:8)

We could safely paraphrase that to say, "*Speak* only those things which are honest, just, pure, of a good report."

False Teachers

Notes

Peter told of false prophets and teachers who invent erroneous doctrines to cause people to support them in the manner to which they have become accustomed. Their teachings are nothing more than lies of Satan.

> *But there were false prophets also among the people, even as there shall be false teachers among you, who privily shall bring in damnable heresies, even denying the Lord that bought them, and bring upon themselves swift destruction. And many shall follow their pernicious ways.* (2 Peter 2:1–2)

The Word of God has to be the final authority if we are going to recognize these frauds. We cannot allow ourselves the luxury of being swayed by their personalities or even their miracles. That will be one of the great attractions of the antichrist and the false prophet.

Make the golden-tongued orators stick to the Word or else cut them off at the pockets. God's people need to wake up and stop bankrolling these agents of Satan.

Deceptions and Delusions

The reason we must be so wary is because we are living in the last days of this age, when deception and delusions will be overpowering. We are to *"stand fast, and hold the traditions which ye have been taught, whether by word, or our epistle"* (2 Thessalonians 2:15).

One of our large crusade churches in Latin America gave us an opportunity to see how subtly lying spirits can slip into a church situation if we are not extremely careful. This particular crusade was the most productive, successful church we had been privileged to build up to that time, and this incident involved the most important leaders of the young church.

One of the interesting customs of Latin American churches is what they call "vigilias," or all-night prayer and praise meetings. In our crusades, we have services every night of the year, so I was less than enthusiastic when some of the new converts came to me with the suggestion that we have a "vigilia" every week. Our schedule was already

NOTES

God's Spirit always speaks in line with His Word.

so jammed with services every night in three church crusades, television and radio programs, and the oversight of construction on the large church buildings that I knew it would be tempting God to go without sleep 24–36 hours at a time each week. Besides, I thought the people were doing well to attend the regular services every night.

But I found it impossible to tell new converts they couldn't pray and praise the Lord. I instructed them that if they would faithfully follow the Word in everything they did, I would allow them to have their vigilias.

A few weeks later, I began hearing rumors of strange activities taking place at the all-night meetings. One of the people I had the most confidence in was giving prophecies that were off the wall. There was one prophecy about an earthquake that would destroy Costa Rica, which did not materialize within the time frame mentioned. They had also been commanded to raise an elderly lady from the dead who had been buried for a year and had died an unbeliever.

It didn't take much investigation to find that, although they had started out correctly, a lying spirit had been allowed to operate in their meetings. The leader apparently was enjoying the sense of power her prophecies gave her in the group. Pride had blinded her to the fact that her prophecies were no longer lining up with God's Word.

God helped us salvage a very difficult situation, for which we give Him all the glory. The new converts came through the experience somewhat scarred, but infinitely wiser. Satan's goal of destroying the new church was stifled.

God Is Truth

The bottom line in all of this is that God's Spirit always speaks in line with what the Word has already stated. There will *never* be a prophecy from God that contradicts the written Word of God. Second, God's prophets are *always 100 percent correct* in their prophecies. Third, God's prophecies always glorify and uplift the name of God, not the human personality that is used to give it. Unless the prophet and the prophecy meet these basic requirements, the prophet is either speaking out of his own spirit or else there is a lying spirit in the works somewhere. There are only three possible spirits that can be involved in prophecy: God's, man's, or a satanic spirit.

Because we follow God's Spirit, we are privileged to have a direct pipeline to the truth. While the rest of the world rushes pell-mell on the road to hell, following the lies of Satan, we can follow Jesus into heavenly places because the truth has made us free. (See John 8:32.)

> *When he, the Spirit of truth, is come, he will guide you into all truth: for he shall not speak of himself; but whatsoever he shall hear, that shall he speak: and he will show you things to come. He shall glorify me: for he shall receive of mine, and shall show it unto you.*
> (John 16:13–14)

God's Word Gives Us Power

We are going to ask God's forgiveness now for those of you who have been believing the lies the devil has been pumping into your minds. The lying strongman has told you vicious lies about your wife, husband, brother-in-Christ, or people you associate with. Others of you he has lied to, saying you have cancer or some other terminal disease, or he has kept you in a constant state of terror as he dangles an impending disaster before your eyes. Some of you have to take pills to calm your anxieties simply because you have believed those terrible lies.

We realize this signifies that we doubt God and His Word. Therefore, we must drive it out of our lives by an act of will and the power of the Spirit of Truth.

Let's Pray

"Father, I approach Your throne of mercy in the blessed name of Jesus. I can see that I've been leaving a door open in my life to the attacks of this lying strongman because of a lack of faith and knowledge of Your Word. Forgive me and help me walk in the freedom of Your truth from this day on.

"Satan, in the name of Jesus I bind you and your lying spirit according to Matthew 18:18, which informs me,

NOTES

NOTES

'Whatsoever ye shall bind on earth shall be bound in heaven.' I close this open door to the lying spirit in my life in the name of Jesus.

"Thank You, Lord, for giving me victory over the lying strongman. According to Matthew 18:18, that promises, *'Whatsoever ye shall loose on earth shall be loosed in heaven,'* I loose the spirit of truth in my life. Help me to read Your Word each day so that I can maintain the dominion over Satan that I need in these last days. Thank You, Lord, for guiding my life and answering my prayer. Amen."

Notes

Perverse Spirit

Isaiah 19:14

Broken Spirit
Proverbs 15:4

Atheist
Proverbs 14:2; Romans 1:30

Evil Actions
Proverbs 17:20, 23

Filthy Mind
Proverbs 2:12; 23:33

Incest

Pornography

Abortion
Exodus 20:13; 21:22–25

Sexual Perversions
Romans 1:17–32; 2 Timothy 3:2

Child Abuse

Chronic Worrier
Proverbs 19:3

Doctrinal Error
Isaiah 19:14; Romans 1:22–23; 2 Timothy 3:7–8

Twisting the Word
Acts 13:10; 2 Peter 2:14

Foolish
Proverbs 1:22; 19:1

Contentious
Philippians 2:14–16; 1 Timothy 6:4–5; Titus 3:10–11

Roots are
"...works of the flesh."
—Galatians 5:19–21

"By their fruits ye shall know them."
—Matthew 7:20

According to Matthew 18:18...

Bind: Perverse Spirit

Loose: God's Spirit, Pureness, Holiness

Zechariah 12:10; Hebrews 10:29

Chapter 5

Perverse Spirit

The Lord hath mingled a perverse spirit in the midst thereof: and they have caused Egypt to err in every work thereof, as a drunken man staggereth in his vomit.
—Isaiah 19:14

Here we have a Scripture that appears to blame God for the actions of a strongman; the mingling of a perverse spirit in the midst of Egypt. But the evidence of God's Word proves that He does not need the help of perverse spirits to accomplish His will on this earth. A better way of interpreting this passage would be that, because of Egypt's continual sin, God took His hands off the situation, allowing the perverse spirit to lead the nation into all kinds of problems.

The straw that broke the proverbial camel's back is found in the third verse, where it says the Egyptians sought the help of idols, charmers, familiar spirits, and wizards. That is an automatic hands-off signal where God is concerned. He will not tolerate divided allegiance.

The first chapter of Romans is the New Testament equivalent of the above mentioned Egyptian debacle, *"And even as they did not like to retain God in their knowledge, God gave them over to a reprobate mind, to do those things which are not convenient"* (Romans 1:28).

When people insist on doing the unnatural, God steps back, and a reprobate mind moves in. In this state, they become so twisted in their thinking process that they believe their lifestyle is actually normal. This attitude is evident in the homosexual community today as they seek respectability for their perverted practices.

God Is Always the Same

But God's Word has not changed; perversion is still perversion. God didn't create two men or two women in

Notes

NOTES

the garden of Eden. He created a man and a woman and blessed that union. That was the prototype of sexual behavior for the human race. Times, customs, and philosophies may have changed since that time, but God's Word has not. Those who obey the Word receive God's blessings, and those who don't not only feel the displeasure of God but also experience the results of their perversion.

> *For this cause God gave them up unto vile affections: for even their women did change the natural use into that which is against nature: and likewise also the men, leaving the natural use of the woman, burned in their lust one toward another; men with men working that which is unseemly, and receiving in themselves that recompense of their error which was meet.* (Romans 1:26–27)

AIDS

A comparatively new disease called AIDS (Acquired Immune Deficiency Syndrome) "has thousands of gay men sweating in terror."[1] Although a few cases have appeared in non-homosexuals, the overwhelming majority have been either homosexuals, bisexual men, or people directly associated with them, such as drug users who injected themselves with the same needles as the homosexuals. Hemophiliacs, dependent upon blood donors to maintain their lives, have also been widely affected.

"Nearly 100 million people worldwide could die from AIDS by the end of the century if a cure or vaccine is not found," says former U.S. Surgeon General, C. Everett Koop. [2]

"Fewer than 14 percent of AIDS victims have survived more than three years after being diagnosed, and no victim has recovered fully." [3]

"The median number of male sexual partners for homosexual patients who contracted AIDS is 1,160."[4]

It appears that medical science is on the road to discovering a vaccine for this dreaded disease, but most reports agree that it will be years before such a vaccine is available. Even then, the vaccine will not cure the thousands who have already contracted AIDS; it only protects those who *do not* have it from contracting AIDS.

Although the plague will have far-reaching effects on humanity, the best way to keep from becoming infected is to live like God's Word says we should live. Those who embrace the new morality and its related branches may scoff at God's Word, but the truth is that those who insist on breaking God's laws receive *"in themselves that recompense of their error"* (Romans 1:27).

Leviticus 20 spells out the gravity of sexual perversion. Homosexuality, incest, adultery, and bestiality were all punishable by death under the law. (See Leviticus 20:10–17.)

The twisted mind of the perverse man or woman is a stronghold of Satan. The perverse strongman delights in seeing how far he can detour mankind from God's blueprint for human conduct. If God's Word commands one thing, the perverse spirit seeks to lead humanity in the exact opposite direction.

Isaiah showed how much Satan has succeeded in doing just that through the centuries.

> *For my thoughts are not your thoughts, neither are your ways my ways, saith the* Lord. *For as the heavens are higher than the earth, so are my ways higher than your ways, and my thoughts than your thoughts.*
> (Isaiah 55:8–9)

Observe the following God-given gifts that man has twisted and perverted: sex, music, earth's environment, philosophy, the family unit, the atom, television, the printed page, appetite for food...the list goes on and on.

Show a group of people a white sheet of paper with a small black mark in the middle and ask them what they see. Ninety-nine percent of them will answer, "A black mark." Occasionally someone will say, "I see a white sheet of paper."

Have you noticed that when people give directions they always tell you to go to the first "red" light? Why don't they send you to the first "green" light?

Why are bars and taverns more successful when the interior lighting is dim? Paul said the reason is that when

Notes

A perverse strongman delights in detouring mankind from God's blueprint.

NOTES

God makes us new creatures when we accept Christ, but our minds must be renewed by the Word.

men *"became vain in their imaginations,...their foolish heart was darkened"* (Romans 1:21).

Man Is Not Synchronized

Unregenerate man is not synchronized with God's universe. Sin has twisted him so that right is wrong, dark is light, a lie is the truth, Satan is credible, and God is out-of-date. Isaiah put it like this: *"Woe unto them that call evil good, and good evil; that put darkness for light, and light for darkness; that put bitter for sweet, and sweet for bitter!"* (Isaiah 5:20).

People who attend our crusades in Latin America tell of parents who would prefer that their children be alcoholics than Protestants. Some Moslems kill family members who accept Christ. Many people in India will not kill rats because of their belief in reincarnation. As a result, the rats eat the food and people starve to death. We are told that mothers in certain parts of Africa have thrown their babies to the crocodiles to appease the demons they serve. Why? Their minds have been darkened and perverted by sin.

Only the light of God's Word can break through such spiritual darkness and reveal their twisted condition. Jesus informed His disciples, as well as the human race in general, *"I am the way, the truth, and the life"* (John 14:6).

God makes us new creatures when we accept Christ as our Savior, but our minds must still be reprogrammed daily by the renewing power of the Word of God (Romans 12:2).

We are to "[cast] *down imaginations, and every high thing that exalteth itself against the knowledge of God, and* [bring] *into captivity every thought to the obedience of Christ"* (2 Corinthians 10:5). Only then can we have the *"sound mind"* that 2 Timothy 1:7 tells us is available to those who do not allow this world to press them into its mold.

Don't allow Satan's followers to give you an inferiority complex. This world is having a gigantic nervous breakdown as it blindly follows Satan, a twisted, perverted lunatic. And *they* have the nerve to say *we* are crazy because we follow Christ! The truth is that it is insane to reject a loving

God who has done everything possible to save mankind from the filthy clutches of the universal pervert, Satan.

Instead of retreating into our plush churches and waiting for Jesus to rapture us out of this lost world, God expects us to attack the ruler of this world as Jesus did on the cross. He cried, *"Father, forgive them; for they know not what they do"* (Luke 23:34). Jesus knew who the real enemy was behind the cross. Those who nailed Him to the cross were only the perverted tools of Satan.

Satan bungled things as usual when he allowed Jesus to enter his private domain by way of death. When the Son of God rose from the dead, He stripped Satan, taking the keys of death and hell with Him. (See Revelation 1:18.)

Now we have been given the power to continue that dominion in the name of Jesus. Instead of bewailing the fact that the world is rotting away, we must apply some of the preservative salt that Jesus says we are to be in this world. (See Matthew 5:13.) Every opportunity you get, take dominion over the perverse spirits in the name of Jesus. Whenever you encounter pornography, abortion, filthy television and movies, homosexuals, lesbians, child abusers, sex clubs, filthy communication, false cults, and perverse speech, you can be assured a perverse strongman is in operation.

Take Dominion!

It is not enough to join a boycott against television sponsors. Until we begin taking dominion over evil in the *spiritual* arena, we will face a lot of frustrations. God has given us the weapons we need to go for the enemy's jugular and bind him where it will do the most good. So let's do it!

If you are tempted in any of these areas, you must go after this strongman aggressively in the name of Jesus. God's children cannot take the risk of allowing such a filthy spirit leeway in their lives. The roots take hold very quickly.

Those of you who have problems with this strongman can pray this prayer of forgiveness with me: "Father, I

NOTES

NOTES

approach You in the name of Jesus. Forgive me for allowing a perverse spirit access to my life. I realize these actions not only place me in spiritual danger but also grieve Your Holy Spirit. I want to please you, Father, with all my heart. Cleanse me from all impurity of mind or deed.

"Satan, in the name of Jesus, I bind your perverse spirit according to Matthew 18:18, which tells me, *'Whatsoever ye shall bind on earth shall be bound in heaven.'* You no longer have an open door in my life through this spirit.

"Thank You, Lord, for giving me freedom over the power of the devil. According to Matthew 18:18, which promises, *'Whatsoever ye shall loose on earth shall be loosed in heaven,'* I loose God's Spirit of grace and supplication, which is the Holy Spirit, to guide me in a life of purity and excellence. Help me to reprogram my mind on a daily basis by reading Your Word. Thank You, Lord, for confirming Your Word in my life. Amen."

Notes

Spirit of Haughtiness (Pride)

Proverbs 16:18

Pride

Proverbs 6:16–17; 16:18–19; 28:25; Isaiah 16:6

Self-Deception

Jeremiah 49:16; Obadiah 1:3

Idleness

Ezekiel 16:49–50

Scornful

Proverbs 1:22; 3:34; 21:24; 24:9; 29:8

Arrogance, Smugness

2 Samuel 22:8; Jeremiah 48:29; Isaiah 2:11, 17; 5:15

Obstinate

Proverbs 29:1; Daniel 5:20

Strife

Proverbs 28:25

Contentious

Proverbs 13:10

Rejection of God

Psalm 10:4; Jeremiah 43:2

Self-Righteous

Luke 18:11–12

Rebellion

1 Samuel 15:23; Proverbs 29:1

Roots are
"...works of the flesh."
—Galatians 5:19–21

"By their fruits ye shall know them."
—Matthew 7:20

According to Matthew 18:18...

Bind: Spirit of Haughtiness (Pride)

Loose: Humble & Contrite Spirit

Proverbs 16:19; Romans 1:4

Chapter 6

Spirit of Haughtiness (Pride)

Pride goeth before destruction,
and an haughty spirit before a fall.
—Proverbs 16:18

We have already noted what happened to Lucifer. He became filled with pride and boasted, *"I will be like the most High"* (Isaiah 14:14). It is not possible to fall any farther than he did—from the most beautiful creation of God to the very pit of hell.

The spirit of haughtiness would like to keep us from becoming the creation God wants to make of us—namely, the best people we can possibly be. And we only realize that objective to the extent that we open ourselves to God and say, "I'm Yours, God, mold and make me into the person You want me to be."

The popular song "I Did It My Way" is the theme song of the self-made, proud, haughty man of the world. When you ask him how he became what he is today, his first word is invariably, *I.* This overexaggerated opinion of himself causes him to believe he does not need the guidance and strength of God. That is dangerous because it opens him up to the operation of a haughty spirit.

The deception in a case like this is that such a person *appears* to be successful. But when you dig down below the outward glitter, there is usually an alcohol, drug, or health problem, a string of broken marriages, and an extremely unhappy, lonely person whose children consider him to be an ogre. Why? Because there is no *true* success apart from doing the will of God.

"By humility and the fear of the Lord are riches, and honour, and life" (Proverbs 22:4).

Notes

NOTES

True humility is recognizing we can do nothing without the help of God.

Jesus said, *"For whosoever exalteth himself shall be abased; and he that humbleth himself shall be exalted"* (Luke 14:11).

"Better it is to be of an humble spirit with the lowly, than to divide the spoil with the proud" (Proverbs 16:19).

Humility is not always easy to define. We jokingly refer to the fellow who wrote the book on humility and how he attained it. Or that someone has a "gift of humility" because they are constantly humiliating everyone around them.

I once knew a man who thought he was humble because he let everyone walk all over him. His wife and children gladly obliged and considered him to be something of a joke because he failed to take his rightful place as head of his household.

Jesus declared that He was *"meek and lowly in heart"* (Matthew 11:29). But we do not consider Him to be weak in any sense of the word. When the occasion called for it, Jesus made a whip and drove the moneychangers out of the temple. The Pharisees never did win an intellectual or Biblical argument with Him. Yet, we recognize that Jesus was the epitome of humility. What was it that made Jesus humble?

Here is the answer, *"I can of mine own self do nothing... because I seek not mine own will, but the will of the Father which hath sent me. I can of mine own self do nothing"* (John 5:30).

TRUE HUMILITY

True humility is recognizing that *"all our righteousnesses are as filthy rags"* (Isaiah 64:6) and that we can do nothing without the help and direction of God in our lives.

Any variance from this divine principle will bring the haughty strongman's influence into our lives to the degree that we think we are capable of running our lives apart from God.

GIVE EVERYTHING TO JESUS

How much better it is to relax and give our lives to God. He is the *only* one who can really make something beautiful out of it anyhow. We can trust God not to take advantage of us when we release our lives into His hands. He will guide us into the exact place where we can develop to our full potential. And the bonus is that we will have peace in our hearts and a sense of fulfillment in our souls while it is all going on.

Oh, there will be problems. But when we have the basic agreement worked out between us and God, as to who the Boss is, it leaves us free to concentrate all of our God-given abilities on the challenges of life. There is no other life that even approaches that of having God as a Senior Partner.

> *Yea, all of you be subject one to another, and be clothed with humility: for God resisteth the proud, and giveth grace to the humble. Humble yourselves therefore under the mighty hand of God, that he may exalt you in due time: casting all your care upon him; for he careth for you.* (1 Peter 5:5–7)

God isn't afraid to exalt us when we are ready for it. That eliminates all the scratching and clawing we feel the successful person must do to climb the ladder of success. We don't sit around feeling frustrated because we aren't becoming the great earth shaker we envisioned ourselves becoming. When we learn what God is teaching us, He will exalt us as we are able to handle it. This makes it possible to appreciate and enjoy what He gives us to the fullest extent.

Paul wrote, *"Eye hath not seen, nor ear heard, neither have entered into the heart of man, the things which God hath prepared for them that love him"* (1 Corinthians 2:9). That isn't just talking about heaven. It also includes the here and now.

The Great Robbery

The haughty spirit attempts to rob us of God's best for our lives. We recognize him either in our own lives or in the lives of others when we encounter the following symptoms: pride, arrogance, contentiousness, scornful anger, obstinance, stubbornness, rebellion, and boastfulness.

Notes

NOTES

Only God can make us into something useful for Him.

Here are some Scriptures that speak of these things.

> *Only by pride cometh contention: but with the well advised is wisdom.* (Proverbs 13:10)
>
> *The lofty looks of man shall be humbled, and the haughtiness of men shall be bowed down, and the LORD alone shall be exalted in that day.* (Isaiah 2:11)
>
> *Proud and haughty scorner is his name, who dealeth in proud wrath.* (Proverbs 21:24)
>
> *For rebellion is as the sin of witchcraft, and stubbornness is as iniquity and idolatry.* (1 Samuel 15:23)
>
> *These six things doth the LORD hate: yea, seven are an abomination unto him: a proud look....* (Proverbs 6:16–17)
>
> *Behold, this was the iniquity of thy sister Sodom, pride, fulness of bread, and abundance of idleness was in her and in her daughters, neither did she strengthen the hand of the poor and needy. And they were haughty, and committed abomination before me: therefore I took them away as I saw good.* (Ezekiel 16:49–50)

When we see these things in our lives, obstructing spiritual progress or trying to take over, we must immediately take the necessary measures to get them out of our lives.

JAMES' ADVICE

James gave some helpful advice when he said, *"Humble yourselves in the sight of the Lord, and he shall lift you up"* (James 4:10). Note that the subject is understood here: "*You* humble yourselves." We are the catalysts in this process. We make up our minds and wills to humbly accept God's will for our lives and then walk in that will, recognizing that only God can make us into something useful for Him.

FORGIVE ME!

We begin by asking God's forgiveness. "Father, I come to You in the name of Jesus. I see that I have not allowed

You to reign supreme in my life. Forgive me for this terrible sin. I humbly bow before You with a contrite spirit and ask that You make something beautiful out of my life."

Bind the Enemy

"Satan, in the name of Jesus, I bind your haughty spirit according to Matthew 18:18, which states, *'Whatsoever ye shall bind on earth shall be bound in heaven.'* I recognize you for what you are—a thief and a robber. I refuse to allow you to lead me away from God's will for my life."

Loose the Spirit of God

"Thank You, Father, for Your forgiveness of this terrible sin. According to Matthew 18:18, which promises, *'Whatsoever ye shall loose on earth shall be loosed in heaven,'* I loose a humble spirit, a spirit of holiness in my life to lead me in the path that You choose for me to walk. I recognize that I can find that path best by reading and studying Your Word, which *'is a lamp unto my feet, and a light unto my path'* (Psalms 119:105). Thank You, Lord, for hearing and answering my prayer. Amen."

Notes

Spirit of Heaviness

Isaiah 61:3

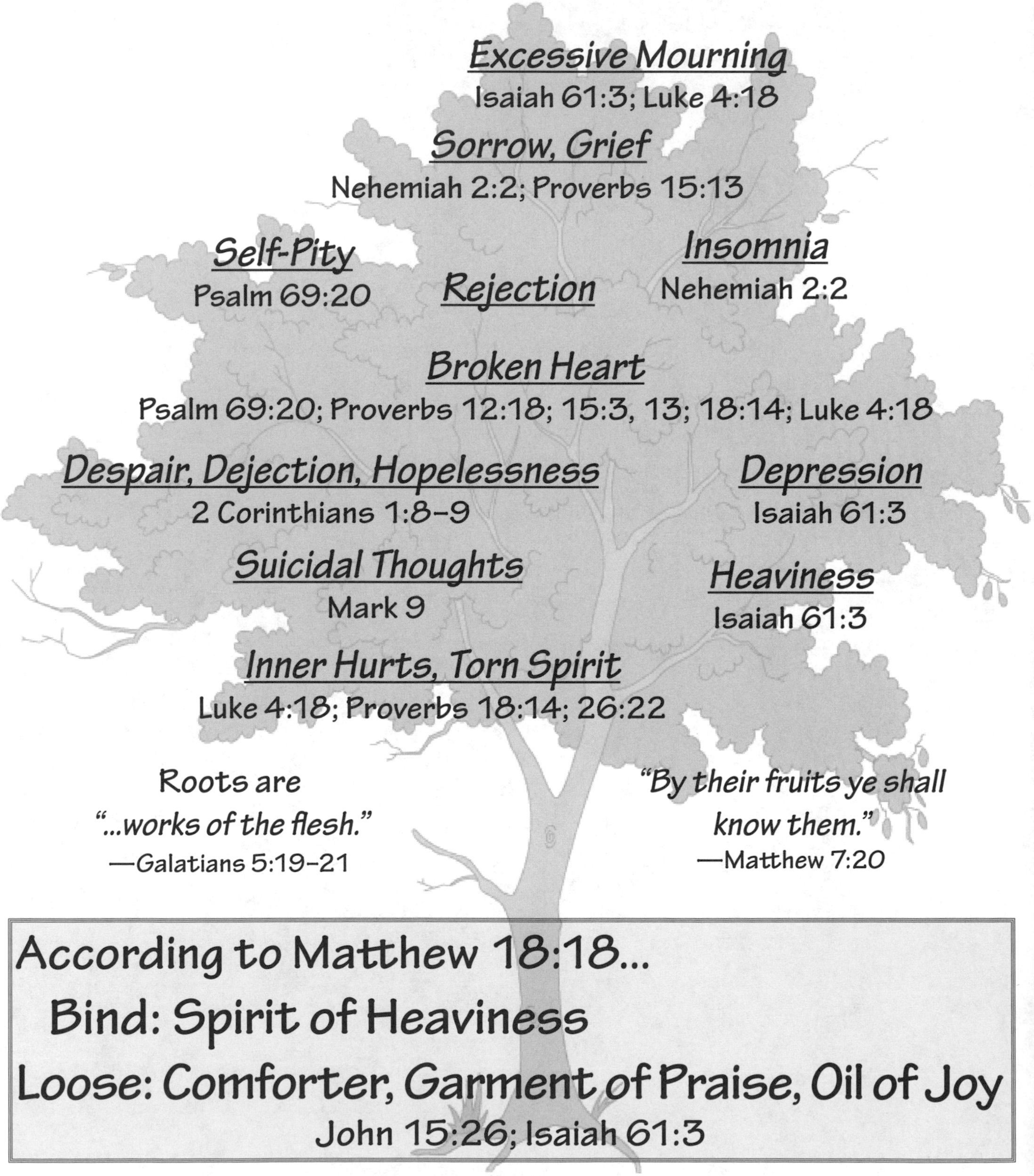

Excessive Mourning
Isaiah 61:3; Luke 4:18

Sorrow, Grief
Nehemiah 2:2; Proverbs 15:13

Self-Pity
Psalm 69:20

Rejection

Insomnia
Nehemiah 2:2

Broken Heart
Psalm 69:20; Proverbs 12:18; 15:3, 13; 18:14; Luke 4:18

Despair, Dejection, Hopelessness
2 Corinthians 1:8–9

Depression
Isaiah 61:3

Suicidal Thoughts
Mark 9

Heaviness
Isaiah 61:3

Inner Hurts, Torn Spirit
Luke 4:18; Proverbs 18:14; 26:22

Roots are
"...works of the flesh."
—Galatians 5:19–21

"By their fruits ye shall know them."
—Matthew 7:20

According to Matthew 18:18...
Bind: Spirit of Heaviness
Loose: Comforter, Garment of Praise, Oil of Joy
John 15:26; Isaiah 61:3

Chapter 7

Spirit of Heaviness

To appoint unto them that mourn in Zion, to give unto them beauty for ashes, the oil of joy for mourning, the garment of praise for the spirit of heaviness.
—Isaiah 61:3

Symptoms

The symptoms of this strongman include, as the text suggests: excessive mourning, sorrow and grief, depression, despair, dejection, hopelessness, self-pity, loneliness, disappointment, insomnia, inner hurts, and bruises. The spirit of heaviness tries to take our joy of living by loading us down with heaviness. He attempts to move in when we are mourning and keep us in an abnormal state of perpetual grief.

Mourning

It is normal and healthy to have a period of mourning after the loss of a loved one, or even a favored possession, job position, pet, boy- or girlfriend. Whenever we lose something that we value highly, it takes time to adjust both physically and psychologically to the vacuum that results. But we do not mourn indefinitely. "Grief is a God-given emotion that allows us to empty out the deep feelings that must not be kept inside; but grief, if long continued, can become a neurotic return to immaturity, and therefore is destructive."[1] We allow the Comforter to heal the hurt and carry away our grief. *"Surely he hath borne our griefs, and carried our sorrows"* (Isaiah 53:4). We release it to the Lord and go on with life as best we can.

I've known people who have lost a loved one and never gotten over it. Twenty-five years later they are still mourning the anniversary of the death as though it had just happened. As a result, all kinds of negative things take place

Notes

NOTES

God wants to turn our "ashes" into something of beauty.

in their lives. The remaining living members of the family resent taking second place to a dead person. The physical health of those involved is affected, and a spirit of fear usually moves in somewhere along the line.

When death is magnified, it creates fear. How many times can we recount the details of how someone died without being affected by the whole process, especially if it was excessively violent or morbid? God's people do not concentrate their attention on death, but on Christ, who is Life. *"But this one thing I do, forgetting those things which are behind, and reaching forth unto those things which are before, I press toward the mark for the prize of the high calling of God in Christ Jesus"* (Philippians 3:13–14).

Isaiah assured us that God wants to turn our "ashes," or death experiences, into something of beauty. He does that when we put on the garment of praise and apply the oil of joy to our aching hearts. We know death isn't a happy experience for anyone, but, to the believer who views it from the perspective of God's Word, it can still make a positive contribution to his growth process in God.

We put on the garment of praise by thanking God for the time He gave us with our loved ones here on earth. If they were Christians, we know they are enjoying the presence of the Lord, and we will see them in a relatively short time in the light of eternity. We reflect on the positive areas of their lives and keep them in our memories, but we absolutely do not allow self-pity to take control of our lives.

SELF-PITY

Self-pity usually results from a selfish motive; we resent the fact that we have been left alone to cope while our loved ones are off walking on the streets of gold. Sometimes self-pity sets in because circumstances or friendships have not worked out the way we had designed for them to work. Loneliness strikes us and we are tempted to retreat into a shell and give up. But remember, all of this is not God working in our lives but the destroyer. Don't let him do it! God has promised to be with us, working everything out for our good (Romans 8:28). *"When thou passest through the waters, I will be with thee; and through the rivers, they shall not overflow thee"* (Isaiah 43:2).

Broken Relationships

Notes

The death of a relationship leaves one or both parties involved reeling from the aftereffects of the hurts. Satan often uses misunderstandings to thrust his fiery darts and cause deep wounds in our spirits and souls. He tries to kill the unity of friends, loved ones, and members of the body of Christ.

Our first response needs to be one of asking forgiveness of God and, if possible, the other person involved. Second, we must forgive the other person by an act of our wills and keep it committed to Christ. We can't afford to go back and play with the details of the problem anymore. We must practice bringing every thought into obedience and thinking only on good reports and pure things.

Binding the work of the enemy and walking out forgiveness is a continual process as God does His healing in our spirits by restoring the wholeness we need. It will often take some time before we stop hurting, but we can be assured that we are not holding anger, guilt, unforgiveness, or any other thing that might open a door of access to the destroyer.

Depression

"Depression is an epidemic that University of Pennsylvania researcher Martin Seligman estimates costs Americans up to *4 billion dollars* in lost work and medical bills. Its social cost is enormous—broken marriages, troubled children, suicide, even homicide.

"The National Institute of Mental Health says one in every five Americans, 40 million people, have significant symptoms of depression at any one time. About 2.4 million of them suffer severe, clinical depression.

"Depression is the oldest known psychiatric disorder. But scientists still don't know what causes it, much less why most of its victims are women."[2]

First Steps

I have found in dealing with Christian people that one of the first steps down the road to depression is a neglect or loss of interest in God's Word. They become so taken

NOTES

up with the process of living that they neglect the basic spiritual exercises that are required of all who wish to maintain their Christian experience. After a time, these people begin to feel the weight of serving because the joy of the Lord has ebbed out of their lives and they are left with the dull mechanics of Christian living. They begin withdrawing from their responsibilities as they retreat behind walls to seek the seclusion they feel is needed. But the withdrawal demands more withdrawal until loneliness becomes a way of life. "It is too much bother to invite people over for dinner anymore." Life takes on a "sameness" that becomes more and more like a dark tunnel without an exit.

SUICIDE

The same schedule, the same disappointments, the same faces, the same noisy children, the same house to clean, the *same* everything. Is there no way out? "Possibly an automobile accident in which I am fatally injured would give me an escape." What a noble exit! Down, down, down goes the mood until the will is paralyzed. Other strongmen move in, and the day comes when everyone is shocked to hear that Sister or Brother So-and-So committed suicide by overdosing on sleeping pills.

In talking with people who tried to kill themselves, they told me they felt a great heaviness pushing them into the act of attempting suicide.

KING SAUL

King Saul was often attacked by depression after the Spirit of God had departed from him. When he couldn't sleep, he would call for David to play beautiful, anointed psalms of praise to God, and the attacks of heaviness would be dispelled. David gained invaluable experience from these episodes that helped him win the victory over depression later in his own life.

The garment of praise is the most effective deterrent against the spirit of heaviness and its related symptoms of insomnia, depression, loneliness, and self-pity. Whenever I have difficulty sleeping, I just start praising the Lord. I tell the devil that if he disturbs my sleep, he will only give me more time to praise the Lord and pray. I can't lose on that one, can I? And the devil soon picks up his toys and leaves.

God inhabits the praises of His people. (See Psalm 22:3.)

> *When the enemy shall come in like a flood, the Spirit of the LORD shall lift up a standard against him.*
> (Isaiah 59:19)

> *Know ye not, that to whom ye yield yourselves servants to obey, his servants ye are to whom ye obey; whether of sin unto death, or of obedience unto righteousness?*
> (Romans 6:16)

Be Aggressive

Be aggressive! Don't yield to those dark moods and depressions. Use the Word of God like the sword that it is to slash away at the enemy who is robbing you of the joy, peace, and contentment that should be yours as a child of God. When the symptoms of depression start, just loose the garment of praise and the oil of joy to cover you from head to toe. Allow praises to flow from your thoughts and mouth. It may require discipline on your part at first but the more you praise God the easier it gets. Use your prayer language. If you haven't received the baptism of the Holy Spirit, make it a priority in your life.

Be Obedient

Why don't we pray now? "Dear God, I come to You in the name of Jesus. I don't especially feel like praying. I'm doing it in obedience to Your Word. Forgive me for neglecting my time of prayer with You and the reading of Your Word. I've allowed the spirit of heaviness to rob me of the good things You have for me. But I promise to reject those thoughts of self-pity and to make praise to You a way of life from this time forward."

Bind the Spirit of Heaviness

"Satan, in the name of Jesus I bind your spirit of heaviness according to Matthew 18:18, which promises, *'Whatsoever ye shall bind on earth shall be bound in heaven.'*

NOTES

The more you praise God, the easier it gets.

NOTES

I recognize that you have taken advantage of me. Now I resist you in the name of Jesus. James 4:7 says, *'Resist the devil, and he will flee from you.'* Go, in the name of Jesus, and don't bother coming back again."

OUR VICTORY

"Thank You, Father, for delivering me from the trap of the enemy. According to Matthew 18:18, which says, *'Watsoever ye shall loose on earth shall be loosed in heaven,'* I loose the Comforter, which is the Holy Spirit, the garment of praise and the oil of joy. I praise Your holy name. Thank You, Jesus, for Your goodness and mercy to me. Thank You for hearing and answering my prayer. Amen."

Notes

Spirit of Whoredoms
Hosea 5:4

Unfaithfulness, Adultery
Ezekiel 16:15, 28; Proverbs 5:1–14; Galatians 5:19

Chronic Dissatisfaction
Ezekiel 16:28

Love of Money
Proverbs 15:27; 1 Timothy 6:7–14

Fornication
Hosea 4:13–19

Idolatry
Judges 2:17; Ezekiel 16; Leviticus 17:7

Spirit, Soul, or Body Prostitution
Ezekiel 16:15, 28; Proverbs 5:1–14; Deuteronomy 23:17–18

Excessive Appetite
1 Corinthians 6:13–16; Philippians 3:19

Worldliness
James 4:4

Roots are
"...works of the flesh."
—Galatians 5:19–21

"By their fruits ye shall know them."
—Matthew 7:20

According to Matthew 18:18...
Bind: Spirit of Whoredoms
Loose: Spirit of God, Pure Spirit
Ephesians 3:6

CHAPTER 8

Spirit of Whoredoms

NOTES

This strongman's name seems to imply that only people who frequent prostitutes are influenced by the spirit of whoredoms. But there is more to it than that. This particular condition can be a *spiritual* bondage, as well as a physical one.

The book of Hosea points out just such a case. *"My people ask counsel at their stocks, and their staff declareth unto them: for the spirit of whoredoms hath caused them to err, and they have gone a whoring from under their God"* (Hosea 4:12).

"They will not frame their doings to turn unto their God: for the spirit of whoredoms is in the midst of them, and they have not known the LORD" (Hosea 5:4).

Hosea's marriage to a harlot illustrated to the nation what they were doing when they forsook God to embrace the idols and false gods of their neighboring nations. Accordingly, Hosea felt the same pain and agony on a physical level with his harlot wife that God experiences when His people are unfaithful to Him in their pursuit of other gods.

Although we may not actually offer sacrifices to a physical idol, whatever comes between us and our relationship to God is still an idol and thus a form of spiritual adultery, although sex may not be involved. Whatever rules us is our god, be it food, sex, diversions, sports, money, power, the pursuit of a career, video games, television, a possession, our children, a religion, or a cause.

TELEVISION

Let us take television as one example. We should be in church on Sunday evening to hear the Word of God, but the best movies are usually run at that time. What comes first? Which is more important in your life?

NOTES

God must take first place in our lives.

Most of us would deny that television is our god because a television junky is considered to be intellectually inferior. But we have noted in our services all over the United States that the Sunday night congregations are usually only half the size of the Sunday morning crowds.

Now the problem on Sunday night may not be television. It could be sports, hunting, fishing, boating, skiing, or a whole bundle of other things. The point is that God has been shifted down the list of priorities until other things now have a dominant place in our lives that they really should not have. Granted, the process is usually very subtle, but the truth is that it *does* happen.

What Dominates You?

Paul made this observation: *"All things are lawful unto me, but all things are not expedient: all things are lawful for me, but I will not be brought under the power of any"* (1 Corinthians 6:12).

Television, sports, food, video games, etc. are not evil in themselves. They only become a problem to us when they dominate our lives. They must be made to take their rightful place way down the list. God is first, our family second, and so on.

> *Love not the world, neither the things that are in the world. If any man love the world, the love of the Father is not in him. For all that is in the world, the lust of the flesh, and the lust of the eyes, and the pride of life, is not of the Father, but is of the world. And the world passeth away, and the lust thereof.* (1 John 2:15–17)

God does not want us to be "spiritual alley cats," chasing whatever pleasure happens to be the latest fad in this world, to the detriment of our spiritual relationship with God. He wants us to be *"redeeming the time, because the days are evil"* (Ephesians 5:16).

Adultery and Fornication

On the other side of the coin, we must be aware that physical adultery and fornication are also the playground of this strongman.

> *Now the body is not for fornication, but for the Lord; and the Lord for the body....Know ye not that your bodies are the members of Christ? shall I then take the members of Christ, and make them the members of an harlot? God forbid....Flee fornication. Every sin that a man doeth is without the body; but he that committeth fornication sinneth against his own body. What? know ye not that your body is the temple of the Holy Ghost which is in you, which ye have of God, and ye are not your own? For ye are bought with a price: therefore glorify God in your body, and in your spirit,* ***which are God's.***
> (1 Corinthians 6:13, 15, 18–20, emphasis added)

Even though extramarital relationships have become the norm in our society, we must understand that God's Word is still the same. Sexual union outside the marriage bond brings bondage and confusion in our lives that chokes out the desire to please God.

We Live by Faith

In this day of fluctuating interest rates and worldwide inflation, God's Word recommends that *"the just shall live by faith"* (Romans 1:17).

> *For we brought nothing into this world, and it is certain we can carry nothing out. And having food and raiment let us be therewith content. But they that will be rich fall into temptation and a snare, and into many foolish and hurtful lusts, which drown men in destruction and perdition. For the love of money is the root of all evil: which while some coveted after, they have erred from the faith, and pierced themselves through with many sorrows. But thou, O man of God, flee these things; and follow after righteousness, godliness, faith, love, patience, meekness. Fight the good fight of faith, lay hold on eternal life, whereunto thou art also called, and hast professed a good profession before many witnesses.* (1 Timothy 6:7–12)

Our most prized possession in this life is our profession of faith. But it can become buried in our drive to pile up money. Jesus said that God clothes the lilies of the field.

Notes

NOTES

Lilies never get uptight worrying about what color they should be or when to open their petals; God cares for them. How much more will He care for us? So just relax. If we want to drive ourselves in search of something, why not go for righteousness, godliness, faith, love, patience, and meekness as Paul suggested above? If we want a good fight, why not the good fight of faith?

GLUTTONY

Gluttony is one sin we hear very little preaching or teaching on these days—probably because we are so busy practicing it. We personally notice it more than the average person because we are constantly being exposed to poverty in the third-world countries where we hold our crusades.

While most of the world is searching for their next meal, we in the U.S. are trying to diet off the excess poundage we have drooping all over our bodies. Sadly, our "temple of the Holy Spirit" is many times composed mostly of lard.

This does not mean we should become obsessed with dieting. But discipline has to extend over into our eating habits, too. Just because the mountain of chocolate is there doesn't mean we have to eat it.

> *For many walk, of whom I have told you often, and now tell you even weeping, that they are the enemies of the cross of Christ: whose end is destruction, whose God is their belly, and whose glory is in their shame, who mind earthly things.* (Philippians 3:18–19)

SPORTS

Something needs to be mentioned about the sports craze that is going on these days. With the advent of all-sports cable television channels, it is possible to spend the rest of your life watching baseball, football, basketball, soccer, and everything in between, down to frog-jumping contests.

Paul's grasp of the sports events of his day reveals that he gave more than a passing glance to them. It is not a sin to go to a ball game or watch it on television, but there is a point we cannot go beyond if we want to maintain a close relationship with God. When I hear pastors bemoan the fact that their church attendance will be low when an important game conflicts with the church service, I know some of God's people are not disciplining their competitive nature.

Sports stadiums today have become religious shrines for millions of people each Sunday. The players are worshipped as some kind of gods for their athletic ability.

Somehow I can't picture true saints of God running around with their mouths hanging open because some guy can kick a pigskin or hit a horsehide ball into the stands.

It's exciting, yes, but there is more to life than that. There is a world out there waiting to be won to Jesus. If you want a challenge, follow me around the countries where the big "wow" in life is the next meal. That puts life into perspective real quick.

> *Therefore, brethren, we are debtors, not to the flesh, to live after the flesh. For if ye live after the flesh, ye shall die: but if ye through the Spirit do mortify the deeds of the body, ye shall live. For as many as are led by the Spirit of God, they are the sons of God.* (Romans 8:12–14)

That is the choice. The flesh or the Spirit; which dominates us? If we have decided to follow Jesus, we dare not entertain the works of the flesh in our lives. They open doors to strongmen spirits who move in to oppress our bodies and souls and eventually our spirits if we do not take appropriate action against them.

Set the Record Right!

"Dear Father, I come to You in the name of Jesus. Forgive me for not keeping You as number one in my life. Forgive me for allowing the works of the flesh and the things of this world to creep in and displace You as the God of my life. I make You Lord of my life, now and forever more, and I promise to follow the instruction of Your Word."

Notes

The flesh or the Spirit; which dominates you?

NOTES

Tear Down Every Idol

"Satan, in the name of Jesus I bind your spirit of whoredoms according to Matthew 18:18, which promises, *'Whatsoever ye shall bind on earth shall be bound in heaven.'* I refuse to allow your paltry imitations of deity to dominate my life. I denounce your idols and rebuke you in the name of Jesus."

Lift Jesus Higher

"Thank You, Father, for delivering me from the gods of this world. According to Matthew 18:18, which states, *'Whatsoever ye shall loose on earth shall be loosed in heaven,'* I loose the Spirit of God in my life. Help me to keep my priorities straight in these confusing days so I will be able to please You and accomplish Your will in my life. Thank You for hearing and answering my prayer. Amen."

Spirit of Infirmity

Luke 13:11–13

Bent Body, Spine
Luke 13:11

Impotent, Frail, Lame
John 5:5; Acts 3:2; 4:9

Asthma, Hay Fever, Allergies
John 5:5

Arthritis
John 5:5

Lingering Disorders
Luke 13:11; John 5:5

Weakness
Luke 13:11; John 5:5

Oppression
Acts 10:38

Cancer
Luke 13:11; John 5:4

Roots are
"...works of the flesh."
—Galatians 5:19–21

"By their fruits ye shall know them."
—Matthew 7:20

According to Matthew 18:18...

Bind: Spirit of Infirmity

Loose: Spirit of Life, Gifts of Healing

Romans 8:2; 1 Corinthians 12:9

Chapter 9

Spirit of Infirmity

We have ministered the Word as missionary evangelists in the areas of faith, healing, and deliverance for many years both in Latin America and the United States. We are convinced, both by the Word of God and by experience, that it is God's will to save, heal, and deliver *anyone* who will accept Christ as the Lord and Savior of his life, believe the Word, live according to the Word, and act on the Word of God with the special faith that comes by hearing God's Word. (See Romans 10:17.)

I remember an elderly lady in Managua, Nicaragua, who came to our open-air crusade. She had been bent double at the waist for twenty years. After accepting the Lord and believing His Word, she was instantly healed and walked back home as straight as everyone else.

A similar healing in the New Testament tells us about the spirit of infirmity.

> *And, behold, there was a woman which had a spirit of infirmity eighteen years, and was bowed together, and could in no wise lift up herself. And when Jesus saw her, he called her to him, and said unto her, Woman, thou art loosed from thine infirmity. And he laid his hands on her: and immediately she was made straight, and glorified God.*
> (Luke 13:11–13)

In verse 16, Jesus spoke even more clearly concerning the cause of the woman's condition. *"And ought not this woman, being a daughter of Abraham, whom Satan hath bound, lo, these eighteen years, be loosed from this bond."*

Luke was careful to note that the spirit of infirmity uses sickness to bind people, thus making those infirmities basically works of Satan.

Notes

NOTES

It is God's will to heal all who are oppressed by the devil.

And having spoiled principalities and powers, he made a show of them openly, triumphing over them in it.
(Colossians 2:15)

INFIRMITY STARTED IN EDEN

In the garden of Eden, God instructed Adam, *"But of the tree of the knowledge of good and evil, thou shalt not eat of it: for in the day that thou eatest thereof thou shalt surely die"* (Genesis 2:17).

When Eve broke the commandment of God and acted as Satan's accomplice in tempting Adam, the results of their sin was death for the entire human race. Adam and Eve died in an instant, spiritually, as sin slashed the cords of fellowship between God and mankind. Physical death was more gradual, as death fastened its tentacles on their bodies for the first time. After a period of centuries, the perfect body that God had fashioned finally succumbed to disease and Adam died.

The ground rules are still the same today. When we obey God's commandments, there is healing for us. If we follow the devil's lies of unbelief and fear, our health will be negatively affected.

Jesus, *"was made in the likeness of men"* (Philippians 2:7), *"took our infirmities, and bare our sicknesses"* (Matthew 8:17), *"and with his stripes we are healed"* (Isaiah 53:5).

Luke mentioned that *"God anointed Jesus of Nazareth with the Holy Ghost and with power: who went about doing good, and healing* ***all*** *that were oppressed of the devil; for God was with him"* (Acts 10:38, emphasis added). You see, it *is* God's will to heal *all* who are oppressed by the devil. Jesus would certainly not do anything against the will of God.

Just as Jesus died on the cross for the sins of the world, so He also paid the price for our healing by receiving the stripes upon His back. It is as unreasonable to believe that God does not want to *save* everyone from their sins as it is to say He does not want to *heal* them of their diseases. The atonement that Jesus provided was a complete work for our bodies, souls, and spirits.

Be Consistent

How strange it is that a Christian who believes God only heals certain people doesn't hesitate to go to the hospital when he is sick. You would think he should stay sick and not go against what he feels is God's will for him.

To overcome that problem, the belief has been taught that God uses sickness to teach His children the lessons they should learn or to discipline them. I always ask those people if they discipline or teach their children by injuring them in some brutal manner. Because they love their children, they are horrified that I would even suggest such a thing. But doesn't God love us too, with an everlasting love? First John 4:16 tells us that, *"God **is** love"* (emphasis added). So how can we attribute to our loving Father such a terrible act as putting a cancer in one of His children; something we could never be capable of doing to our own children? Friend, that is not the kind of God we serve.

What Is God Really Like?

One day, the disciples asked Jesus what God the Father was like. Jesus was astonished. *"Have I been so long time with you, and yet hast thou not known me...? he that hath seen me hath seen the Father"* (John 14:9). Jesus came to clarify the Old Testament view of God the Father: *"Every good gift and every perfect gift is from above, and cometh down from the Father of lights, with whom is no variableness, neither shadow of turning"* (James 1:17).

"I am come that they might have life, and that they might have it more abundantly" (John 10:10). That is what God wants to do in our lives.

Jesus died for our sins so we would not have to die. He took our infirmities so we would not have to be sick.

Why Some Have Difficulty Receiving Healing

Then why aren't some Christians healed? The answer is as varied as the number of believers who are seemingly not healed. Here are a few of the general reasons to be used *only* as your own *personal* checklist:

Notes

God loves us with an everlasting love.

NOTES

(1) Unconfessed sin in the Christian's life.

> *If I regard iniquity in my heart, the Lord will not hear me.* (Psalm 66:18)

> *Wherefore whosoever shall eat this bread, and drink this cup of the Lord, unworthily, shall be guilty of the body and blood of the Lord. But let a man examine himself, and so let him eat of that bread, and drink of that cup. For he that eateth and drinketh unworthily, eateth and drinketh damnation to himself, not discerning the Lord's body. For this cause many are weak and sickly among you, and many sleep* [died prematurely]. (1 Corinthians 11:27–30)

(2) Fear of a certain illness such as cancer that has opened the door to the spirit of infirmity.

(3) Unbelief or ignorance of the Word of God.

(4) A breakdown of the body or mind because they have been abused by an unrealistic workload or lack of proper rest and nutrition.

(5) Hereditary weaknesses or diseases that are innocently accepted because the Christian is unaware of his rights as a child of God.

(6) Some people subconsciously desire to be sick for various illogical reasons.

(7) People continue to walk in the flesh instead of the spirit.

> *Now the works of the flesh are manifest, which are these; adultery, fornication, uncleanness, lasciviousness, idolatry, witchcraft, hatred, variance, emulations, wrath, strife, seditions, heresies, envyings, murders, drunkenness, revellings, and such like: of the which I tell you before, as I have also told you in time past, that they which do such things shall not inherit the kingdom of God.* (Galatians 5:19–21)

The church can pray for people with any of the above problems, but they will not be healed until the problem is resolved correctly, even though the person may outwardly appear to have it all together. God is bound by His Word, and many of His promises are conditional. When we obey and believe the Word and act on what it says, we receive the answer exactly as the Word promises.

God is not willing that *any soul* should perish, but they will, in spite of God's intense desire that they be saved, unless they hear about Jesus and accept Him as their Savior *exactly* as the Word instructs them.

If you have gone through the above checklist and have found that all the doors are truly closed, then the devil is trespassing in your life. Stand on the Word and claim your healing according to God's Word.

Some Ways God Heals

1. **Anointing with Oil—The Prayer of Faith**

> *Is any sick among you? let him call for the elders of the church; and let them pray over him, anointing him with oil in the name of the Lord: and the prayer of faith shall save the sick, and the Lord shall raise him up.* (James 5:14–15)

When the oil touches the forehead, the individual releases his faith to receive healing in that moment.

2. **Agreement**

> *If two of you shall agree on earth as touching any thing that they shall ask, it shall be done for them of my Father which is in heaven. For where two or three are gathered together in my name, there am I in the midst of them.* (Matthew 18:19–20)

The point of contact here is *agreement*. Make sure you tell those who are praying with you exactly what you want them to agree with you about. If they are praying for one thing and you another, there is no agreement. Of course the "anything" mentioned in verse 19 includes healing.

3. **Laying on of Hands**

> *And these signs shall follow them that believe; In my name shall they...lay hands on the sick, and they shall recover.* (Mark 16:17–18)

Many think that only super-spiritual giants of faith are involved in this kind of ministry, but Jesus simply said

NOTES

NOTES

that any believer who *believes* can have these kinds of results. In fact, *all* healthy believers should have these signs following them. That is what this world is crying for today, believers who truly believe God's Word and act on it.

4. **Gifts of Healing**

> *For to one is given by the Spirit the word of wisdom; to another the word of knowledge by the same Spirit; to another faith by the same Spirit; to another the gifts of healing by the same Spirit...but all these worketh that one and the selfsame Spirit, dividing to every man severally as he will.* (1 Corinthians 12:8–9, 11)

There are Christians who mistakenly believe that if they can just be prayed for by someone with the gifts of healing operating in their ministry, they will be healed. But that is not necessarily the case. They may be healed, but then again they may not. The gifts only operate as the Spirit divides them.

The gifts of healing operate differently from the other ways God uses to heal. Matthew 7:7, 11 says,

> *Ask, and it shall be given you; seek, and ye shall find; knock, and it shall be opened unto you: for every one that asketh receiveth....If ye then, being evil, know how to give good gifts unto your children, how much more shall your Father which is in heaven give good things to them that ask him?*

As believers, we *receive by faith* what our Father has promised us in His Word, which certainly includes divine healing. This is God's way of providing healing to the members of the body of Christ.

But, through the gifts of healing, people can be healed whether they meet the usual conditions of healing or not, whether they are saved or not, even whether they want to or not. It is as the Spirit wills.

A lady in Costa Rica openly ridiculed Carol when she told her God could heal her arthritis. After prayer, to the lady's surprise, her twisted fingers began straightening out before her very eyes. She later called in despair because she received disability payments from the government and she was afraid of losing them now that she was

NOTES

healed. The gifts of healing are usually a "sign" miracle to show the power, love, and mercy of God to those involved directly and to the world in general. The gifts are not subject to the human agents through which they flow. He cannot turn them on or shut them off whenever he wants. We just praise the Lord for what is accomplished as the Holy Spirit does what He wants done.

How many times did Jesus pass the lame man at the gate Beautiful and never healed him? (See Acts 3:1–10; 4:1–4.) But one day when Peter and John entered the gate, the Holy Spirit began working. A number of things took place as a result.

(1) The man, lame from his mother's womb, was instantly healed although the only faith he demonstrated was to receive an alms.

(2) The onlookers saw what happened and, *"were filled with wonder and amazement at that which had happened unto him"* (verse 10).

(3) The people rushed to the scene, giving Peter an instant audience to whom he preached the gospel.

(4) As a result of hearing the Word, five thousand men believed on Christ.

(5) The news of the power of Christ spread throughout the region. We desperately need this kind of Holy Spirit activity in our world today to show that God is still the true and living God.

First Corinthians 14:1 instructs that we should *desire* spiritual gifts. Without them, we are just another religion.

5. **When You Pray, Believe That You Receive It.**

"Therefore I say unto you, What things soever ye desire, when ye pray, believe that ye receive them, and ye shall have them" (Mark 11:24). It is understood that *"What things soever ye desire"* includes divine healing.

I believe this is the way mature Christians in the faith should receive healing. There is no need for oil or agreement or laying on of hands, all of which are absolutely correct and proper in God's Word. But what happens if no one is around to do those things for us when the need arises?

NOTES

We teach our new converts in the crusades in Latin America that they are responsible for having sufficient faith to receive the promises of God whether a fellow believer is present or not. I would ask them, "What would you do if you were working alone picking coffee beans and a coral snake bit you on the toe?" (The coral snake bite is deadly, and the action of the venom begins in only ten seconds.) Then I would instruct them, "You had better have faith that works in ten seconds or you will either be dead or, at the very least, lose your leg." I was amazed at the faith they developed in their hearts as they listened night after night to the Word of God.

I remember a lady in the first church we pastored in Oregon who was cleaning her cupboards when a black widow spider bit her. Instantly the Scripture in Mark 16:18 flashed across her spirit, *"They shall take up serpents; and if they drink any deadly thing, it shall not hurt them."* She rebuked it in the name of Jesus and suffered no lasting effects whatsoever!

This is not fantasy we are talking about but basic, New Testament teaching that is needed in each believer's life today. The sad fact is that many have slipped so far from the truth of God's Word that information of this kind is looked at with skepticism and outright disbelief. Can we not see the deception of the enemy? At a time when we need more teaching and preaching about faith than at any other time in history, we are spending our time quibbling over which faith teaching is more correct, theirs or ours. Meanwhile the world is crying out for anything that will stop the forces of evil from chewing them up.

God help us to rise above our pettiness and reach this world with the gospel.

WON'T WE EVER DIE?

"If it is true that God wants to heal everyone who meets the conditions in God's Word, then we would never die," someone suggests. Yes, we will die because the Word says, *"It is appointed unto men once to die"* (Hebrews 9:27). Death is the only way, short of the rapture, that we can get free of this sinful body and into the eternal one that God has prepared for the new creature He created out of us when we accepted Christ as our Savior.

Until that day comes, divine healing is a foreshadow of the perfect health we will have throughout eternity. We live our lives out to the very moment God has chosen to take us home to be with Him—not one minute before or one minute late.

Death has no sting, so it is merely a promotion from earth to heaven. (See 1 Corinthians 15:55.) But while we live in this earthly shell, God has provided for our health.

NOTES

Divine healing is a foreshadow of the perfect health we will have in heaven.

What about Persecutions?

Paul's famous thorn in the flesh was nothing more than persecution: *"And lest I should be exalted above measure through the abundance of the revelations, there was given to me a thorn in the flesh,* ***the messenger of Satan to buffet me,*** *lest I should be exalted above measure"* (2 Corinthians 12:7, emphasis added). In *A Critical Lexicon and Concordance to the English and Greek New Testament,* page 119, the word, *"buffet"* is translated, "to strike with the hands, the fingers being clenched." In 2 Corinthians 11:24–30, Paul gave a rundown of the times he was beaten, stoned, shipwrecked, etc., which certainly puts him in the running for the world's championship of those who are mistreated for Christ's sake.

This is not to say that Paul or his fellow ministers were never sick. They had to apply the healing that Christ accomplished to their bodies just like we do today. But Paul did not succumb to them. He exalted, *"Nay, in all these things we are more than conquerors through him that loved us"* (Romans 8:37).

Check your own life to make sure there isn't an area you have left open for the devil to establish a toehold. If there is, deal with it according to the Word and then confidently rest your life on the promises of God. Sometimes the miracle comes immediately, as we would all rather have it happen. But most of the time the healing takes place gradually, step-by-step as we walk the path of faith.

If there are no openings in your life, you can then be sure the devil is just trying to take advantage of you, and

NOTES

you have every right to resist him in the name of Jesus, claiming your healing according to the promises of God. At times the devil hassles us just because he enjoys it.

Medicine Is Not a Sin

It is not a sin to take medicine until such time as you are able to receive your complete healing. Doctors have been given amazing abilities by God to help in the fight against diseases. But, because mistakes can be made, it is not always wise to put *complete* faith in medical science because mistakes can be made. As children of God, we have access to a higher power that has promised to heal us no matter what the medical diagnosis may be.

Make sure you do your part in strengthening your faith. *"So then faith cometh by hearing, and hearing by the word of God"* (Romans 10:17). The more we open our hearts to the Word of God as it is spoken, the stronger our faith becomes until the day arrives when our bodies react *against* the medicine and there is no doubt that we are healed. Others are prompted by the Holy Spirit to ask for more X-rays because they know the healing is complete despite the fact that some symptoms still remain. Whatever the Holy Spirit leads us to do is what we should do. Just be sure it is the Holy Spirit speaking to your *spirit,* not your mind, and that it is according to God's Word. I have found that when the Holy Spirit speaks there is a *complete* confidence, *without any doubt whatsoever,* that the healing has taken place.

Sometimes it is wise to go back to your doctor and have him reduce the dosage of medicines to proper levels as the healing process is taking place. *All* healings will stand up to a medical exam.

Lingering Illness

The spirit of infirmity seems to be involved with lingering, chronic types of illnesses. John related the story of a man with such a problem.

> *And a certain man was there, which had an infirmity thirty and eight years. When Jesus saw him lie, and knew that he had been now a long time in that case,*

> *he saith unto him, Wilt thou be made whole? The impotent man answered him, Sir, I have no man, when the water is troubled, to put me into the pool: but while I am coming, another steppeth down before me. Jesus saith unto him, Rise, take up thy bed, and walk. And immediately the man was made whole, and took up his bed, and walked.* (John 5:5–9)

The words *"infirmity"* and *"impotent"* suggest a weakness, feebleness, and lack of strength such as a bedridden, chronically ill person would experience.

The name of this strongman in language other than the King James would probably be rendered, "a spirit of disease," which covers most sickness in general. But the protracted types of illnesses are the ones that usually concern us because the person is not able to totally regain his strength once the disease sets in—diseases such as cancer, arthritis, allergies, muscular dystrophy, varieties of sclerosis, heart trouble, asthma, eczema, emphysema, glaucoma, hemophilia, poliomyelitis, diabetes, tetanus, migraine headaches, osteomyelitis, Parkinson's disease, rheumatic fever, and tuberculosis. Of course this is not a complete list, but it does give a general idea of what we are talking about.

The Heavenly Blood Transfusion

Notice that many of the above diseases are hereditary or family weaknesses passed from one generation to the next. But remember that we do not have to automatically receive them just because we belong to a certain bloodline. Resist those family "bugs" in the name of Jesus. We have had a heavenly "blood transfusion," and we now belong to the family of God.

Pray without Fear

Don't be afraid to pray for someone with a dreaded disease if you believe God's Word is true. Jesus told the disciples, *"Behold, I give unto you power to tread on serpents and scorpions, and over all the power of the enemy: and nothing shall by any means hurt you"* (Luke 10:19). Satan will fear *us* when we speak according to God's Word with faith in our hearts and are members of the royal family of God.

Notes

We have had a heavenly "blood transfusion," and we now belong to the family of God.

NOTES

When I pray for someone with cancer, for example, I rebuke and bind the spirit of infirmity that is trying to destroy the cells of his body. Then, I loose the spirit of life into his body and command every cell to become a healthy, vibrant, living cell to the glory of God.

The Prayer of Faith

Now, for those of you who are suffering in your bodies, let us pray the prayer of faith, "Father, in the name of Jesus I come to You boldly as You instructed me to do in Hebrews 4:16. I thank You for Your healing power that is as strong today as it has ever been. I receive Your healing right now by faith in Your Word. I believe that You took my infirmities and bore my sicknesses. By Your stripes *I am healed*."

Bind the Enemy

"In the name of Jesus, I bind the spirit of infirmity according to Matthew 18:18, which says, '*Whatsoever ye bind on earth shall be bound in heaven.*' I demand that you leave me alone and never return to harass me again, in the name of Jesus Christ of Nazareth."

Loose the Power of God

"Thank You, Jesus, for healing me. I loose the spirit of life into every cell of my body, according to Matthew 18:18, which promises, '*Whatsoever ye shall loose on earth shall be loosed in heaven.*' I promise to listen to Your Word so my faith will be strong and grow. I will continually praise You for healing me from this day on. Amen."

Notes

Dumb and Deaf Spirit

Mark 9:17–29

Dumb, Mute
Mark 9:25;
Matthew 9:32–33; 12:22; 15:30–31;
Luke 11:14; Isaiah 35:5–6

Ear Problems
Mark 9: 25–26

Crying
Mark 9:26

Drowning
Mark 9:22

Blindness
Matthew 12:22

Mental Illness
Matthew 17:15; Mark 5:5, 9:17

Suicidal
Mark 9:22

Foaming at the Mouth
Mark 9:39; Luke 9:39

Tearing
Mark 9:18, 20, 26

Burn
Mark 9:22

Gnashing Teeth
Mark 9:18

Seizures, Epilepsy
Mark 9:18, 20, 26

Pining Away
Mark 9:18

Prostration
Mark 9:26

Roots are
"...works of the flesh."
—Galatians 5:19–21

"By their fruits ye shall know them."
—Matthew 7:20

According to Matthew 18:18...
Bind: Dumb and Deaf Spirit
Loose: Resurrection Spirit, Gifts of Healing
Romans 8:11; 1 Corinthians 12:9

Chapter 10

Dumb and Deaf Spirit

As you read this book, do not allow the devil to use a spirit of fear to frighten you. If you sense fear manifesting itself, just stop and rebuke it in the name of Jesus. Satan would like to keep us ignorant of the power we have at our disposal to use against his kingdom. So just relax and learn what God's Word has to say.

Dumb and Deaf

The setting from which we get the name of this strongman is taken from the ninth chapter of Mark.

> *And one of the multitude answered and said, Master, I have brought unto thee my son, which hath a dumb spirit; and wheresoever he taketh him, he teareth him: and he foameth, and gnasheth with his teeth, and pineth away: and I spake to thy disciples that they should cast him out; and they could not. He answereth him, and saith, O faithless generation, how long shall I be with you? how long shall I suffer you? bring him unto me. And they brought him unto him: and when he saw him, straightway the spirit tare him; and he fell on the ground, and wallowed foaming. And he asked his father, How long is it ago since this came unto him? And he said, Of a child. And ofttimes it hath cast him into the fire, and into the waters, to destroy him: but if thou canst do any thing, have compassion on us, and help us. Jesus said unto him, If thou canst believe, all things are possible to him that believeth. And straightway the father of the child cried out, and said with tears, Lord, I believe; help thou mine unbelief. When Jesus saw that the people came running together, he rebuked the foul spirit, saying unto him, Thou dumb and deaf spirit, I charge thee, come out of him, and enter no more into him. And the spirit cried, and rent him*

Notes

NOTES

We can fearlessly dominate Satan in the name of Jesus.

> *sore, and came out of him: and he was as one dead; insomuch that many said, He is dead. But Jesus took him by the hand, and lifted him up; and he arose. And when he was come into the house, his disciples asked him privately, Why could not we cast him out? And he said unto them, This kind can come forth by nothing, but by prayer and fasting.* (Mark 9:17–29)

It is not difficult to recognize that this is a clear-cut case of demon *possession.* It is obvious that the boy was forced by the demon to act contrary to normal human behavior.

Dumb, but Not Stupid

We have found that demons invariably make people do offbeat things because Satan is basically dumb. He *actually* thought he was capable of dethroning God, which is definitely not using good sense. This does not mean that we can relax our defenses against him, for Satan still has vast knowledge of human nature that he can use to our disadvantage. But neither should we give him more credit than he deserves.

Just analyze what people do under the influence of the devil. They make weird noises and do weird things. If everyone else is dressed, they want to take their clothes off. If the situation calls for quiet, they are loud and vice versa. In our crusades, we have had to station people on either side of the platform to keep the drunks from forcing their way to the microphone to say something dumb.

It is dumb for someone to suck smoke out of a white cylinder and get lung cancer. It is dumb for people to drink alcoholic beverages until they can't see straight and then get into their automobiles and kill 25,000 people every year in the United States alone.

Jesus Brings Liberty

Jesus came *"that he might destroy the works of the devil"* (1 John 3:8). Because He accomplished that, we can now fearlessly dominate Satan in the name of Jesus. We have seen many people, who were formerly under Satan's control, suddenly start behaving like normal human beings again when he was commanded to depart in the all-powerful name of Jesus.

NOTES

Our Authority

Before ascending into heaven, Jesus gave a brief job description of what His body of believers would accomplish as He worked with them, confirming His Word with signs following. *"In my name shall they cast out devils; they shall speak with new tongues; they shall take up serpents; and if they drink any deadly thing, it shall not hurt them; they shall lay hands on the sick, and they shall recover"* (Mark 16:17–18).

We do not go around looking for demons to cast out any more than we would look for serpents to handle as some people mistakenly do. But when we *do* encounter the works of Satan in the area of life God has assigned us to, we deal with them in a scriptural manner, and the demons must obey.

We mentioned earlier that there are varying stages of harassment and oppression that can lead to the final state of actual possession, so of course the way in which we deal with each situation will vary accordingly. In the case of the demon-possessed boy, Jesus could not lead him in a prayer of deliverance because he was incapable of following directions.

Demons Lie

Note that Jesus never carried on extensive dialogue with demons and, with only one exception, usually commanded them to be quiet. I personally do not get a special thrill out of talking with demons. They are filthy beings and do not speak the truth, so why even bother? Jesus said that Satan is the father of all lies. We are to cast demons out, not carry on conversations with them.

It should be noted that the only time Jesus asked a demon his name he lied to Jesus! He said his name was *"Legion"* which is the number 6,000 (Mark 5:9). Possibly he was trying to scare Jesus with the huge number of demons, but it didn't work. It just took one Jesus to get rid of the whole pack of them. The point is that if the demon

NOTES

Christian parents should provide a covering for their children.

sidestepped the issue or lied to Jesus, he will do the same to us also.

Jesus' Method

When Jesus saw the crowd running over to gawk at the boy as he was stricken by the demon, He quickly dispensed with the evil spirit. He didn't allow the demon to create a circus atmosphere. One of the reasons for this study is to help us quickly note the exact area of demonic activity and then rout the enemy quickly and efficiently with a minimum of evil manifestation. When Jesus called the demon by name and commanded it to come out and never return, the demonic performance came to a screeching halt.

If information is needed concerning the symptoms, as the case may be when dealing with a troubled child, ask the parents, but then get on with it. Their description will help you locate its scriptural name, and the Holy Spirit will also be there to confirm it in your spirit. If you know the strongman's name, you don't need to spend time binding all the minor spirits under his control. They automatically have to bow their knees and leave.

It is wise to deal with an individual in a room apart from those not directly involved in the situation. It will cut down on the distractions.

Children Can Be Harassed

This demon-possessed boy also demonstrates that children can be bothered and even possessed by demons in extreme cases, usually because the parents or grandparents have been involved in the occult. As we mentioned at the beginning of the book, Satan feels he has the right to do this because of the family involvement in demonic activities. Only after the open door has been closed by the parents can the child be delivered. This boy's father brought him to Jesus, asking for deliverance. When Jesus told him he must cooperate in the matter, he cried out in tears, *"Lord, I believe; help thou mine unbelief"* (Mark 9:24).

Spiritual Covering

We, as Christian parents, should provide a spiritual covering over our children that will protect them from the enemy while they are under our care. Why not deal with rebellion and stubbornness on a spiritual level while they are still babies? Why wait until the teen years before we confront the problem? Our children's survival in this ungodly world may depend upon our taking dominion over the evil forces that would like to snatch them away from under our very noses. We command the forces of evil on a daily basis to leave our children alone.

Of course we must apply discipline on a physical level when it is necessary, just as the Bible instructs. We are to *"train up a child in the way he should go: and when he is old, he will not depart from it"* (Proverbs 22:6).

If we have done all of the above, we can rest on the promises of the Word that our children will serve God. But if we are negligent in any of these parental obligations, spiritual covering, physical discipline, or biblical training, we will be asking for trouble.

Symptoms

The symptoms of this strongman could well describe *some* forms of epilepsy: foaming, gnashing, pining away, falling on the ground violently. In our crusades I cannot remember one case of epilepsy that has not been healed *if they remained to hear the Word over a period of time.*

This is a very important point in deliverance from any kind of demonic attack: the person must continue hearing the Word to build up spiritual strength so he can resist the demons when they try to return, as they *always* will (Matthew 12:43–45). It is not enough to just cast demons out, we must also get the Word of God into the individual and have them receive the baptism of the Holy Spirit as soon as possible. This is why the person who needs deliverance must have a spark of desire to be free and cooperate if the deliverance is to be successful. Otherwise, the demons will make a revolving door out of the poor fellow, *"and the last state of that man is worse than the first"* (Luke 11:26).

Epileptics

I remember a young lady in Costa Rica who had up to seventy epileptic attacks a day. On one occasion, her

Notes

NOTES

husband came home just in time to keep her from feeding poison to her baby, thinking it was milk. After a period of faithfully hearing the Word, her attacks dwindled down to nothing and she was free.

Another girl in the same crusade would fall into a spell of some kind whenever we started praying for the sick and awaken as soon as we were done. One Sunday morning, I felt led of the Lord to bind that spirit in the name of Jesus, and I told the people she would never have an attack again as long as she continued hearing the Word of God. On a number of occasions before coming to the crusade, seven demons appeared to her, telling her to kill her nephew. The whole neighborhood could hear her screams when this would happen. But she was delivered in an instant!

Suicidal

Another symptom of this strongman is suicidal tendencies. *"It...cast him into the fire, and into the waters, to destroy him"* (Mark 9:22).

Suicide can result from a number of factors. In some cases, a lying spirit or a spirit of heaviness or a combination of the two will tell the victim that life isn't worth living and *suggest* that he end it all. Then, there is this kind of spirit that tries to forcibly kill the victim. Of this we can be certain, however, whenever suicide is attempted, it is the handiwork of a satanic strongman because killing is the occupation of the destroyer (John 10:10).

Luke added a detail to this account that is important. *"And as he was yet a coming, the devil threw him down, and tare him. And Jesus rebuked the unclean spirit,* ***and*** *healed the child"* (Luke 9:42, emphasis added).

It appears that, after the demon was cast out it was still necessary for Jesus to heal the boy because of the violence done to the boy by the demon. We could compare this situation to an automobile that has been abused by a driver that hot rods around, "burning rubber" every time he accelerates, taking corners "on two wheels."

When you purchase his car, you have delivered it out of his hands, but there are still repairs that must be done to bring the car back to top condition. Such was the case

NOTES

with this boy. Remember that the loosing of the Holy Spirit is just as important, if not more so, as the binding of the devil. In this case, healing was loosed in the boy.

Here in the United States, we do not usually run into these violent cases because they have already been committed to mental institutions. Drugs are administered, and the individual is so sedated that the demons cannot operate through him.

We are not intimating that every mental patient is demon possessed, because there are mental problems caused by other reasons, such as accidents, problems at birth, etc. But when the demonic symptoms *are* evident, we deal with them in the name of Jesus and get results. For the other types of mental illnesses, we pray the prayer of faith for their healings as we are also instructed in the Word of God.

Blind and Dumb

Another instance where it is specifically recorded that a demon was the cause of a similar problem is found in Matthew 12:22. *"Then was brought unto him one possessed with a devil, blind, and dumb: and he healed him, insomuch that the* ***blind*** *and* ***dumb*** *both spake and saw"* (emphasis added).

During some special services in Portland, Oregon, I prayed for a lady who had suffered from a damaged eye. The doctors had implanted some kind of synthetic material in her eye to alleviate the problem and at the same time correct the vision. It had torn loose, and the lady was in need of more surgery to correct the difficulty. I bound the dumb and deaf spirit that was oppressing her in the name of Jesus. Then I asked the lady if she wanted God to heal what was there or to create a new part in her eye.

"Oh, if God is going to do it," she exclaimed, "I would rather have a new part, not just a repair job!"

So I prayed, "Father, we ask You to create in her eyeball the part that is defective, and I loose Your Spirit of Life in this eye."

"Oh, I can see," she cried. "It's becoming clearer all the time. I see the synthetic piece dissolving, and now it's gone. I can see perfectly!"

NOTES

Another lady could not hear out of one ear. Once again I bound the dumb and deaf spirit that had been oppressing her in the name of Jesus. Then I asked that her ear be made perfectly whole.

When I took my finger out of her ear, I told her that she was healed by faith in the Word. She could hear somewhat better, but her total hearing had not been restored. But we do not walk by what we feel, but by faith in the Word. So I told the lady that, by the time she left the room, she would be hearing perfectly and that she should go away rejoicing and praising the Lord for her total healing.

A few minutes later we heard a loud, "Praise the Lord!" It was the same lady.

She testified that as she walked toward the back of the room praising the Lord, something popped in her ear. "It was just like somebody had pulled a cork out, and now I can hear great!"

Mental Problems

A woman in Oregon came across my path who had been declared a hopeless paranoid. The doctors kept her heavily drugged to maintain a semblance of sanity. I began sharing the Scriptures about healing with her each week and praying for her need. After a few weeks, the caseworker asked me to document what I was doing because they had been able to take her off all the heavy drugs. Her return to health had been so phenomenal they wanted to copy my method!

Prayer and Fasting

Mark ended the account in chapter 9 with the disciples asking Jesus why they couldn't cast the demon out. Jesus had already pinpointed part of the problem in verse 19 as a lack of faith. Some translators mention that Jesus then answered, *"This kind can come forth by nothing, but by prayer and fasting"* (verse 29).

There is no doubt that we must live close to the Lord at all times when we are involved in this kind of ministry. If our bodies are dominating us so that we cannot hear the voice of the Spirit when He speaks to us, we should discipline our bodies by going without food so that they will learn to be quiet when God speaks. And our prayer lives must be kept current at all times.

But do not allow Satan to browbeat you by saying that because you have not fasted forty days you do not have the power to command him to leave in the name of Jesus. We are not doing it in our *own* name and power, but in the *name* and *power* of *Jesus Christ*. Jesus promised, *"If thou canst believe, all things are possible"* (verse 23). So take your liberty in the name of Jesus and do the wonders and exploits that Jesus expects us to do.

NOTES

PRAYER

"Thank You, Father, that Your Word is the truth. We can count on the confirmation of Your Word at all times as we believe and act upon it.

"Satan, in the name of Jesus I bind your dumb and deaf spirit according to Matthew 18:18, which tells me, *'Whatsoever ye shall bind on earth shall be bound in heaven.'* I demand that you stop harassing me this instant. Leave me and never return, you foul spirit.

"Thank You, Jesus, for giving me freedom from all the forces of the enemy. I loose Your Holy Spirit in my life according to Matthew 18:18, which states, *'Whatsoever ye shall loose on earth shall be loosed in heaven.'* I loose resurrection life and the gifts of healings to do a complete work in my body and soul. And I appropriate Your victory over Satan in every area of my life. Amen."

Spirit of Bondage

Romans 8:15

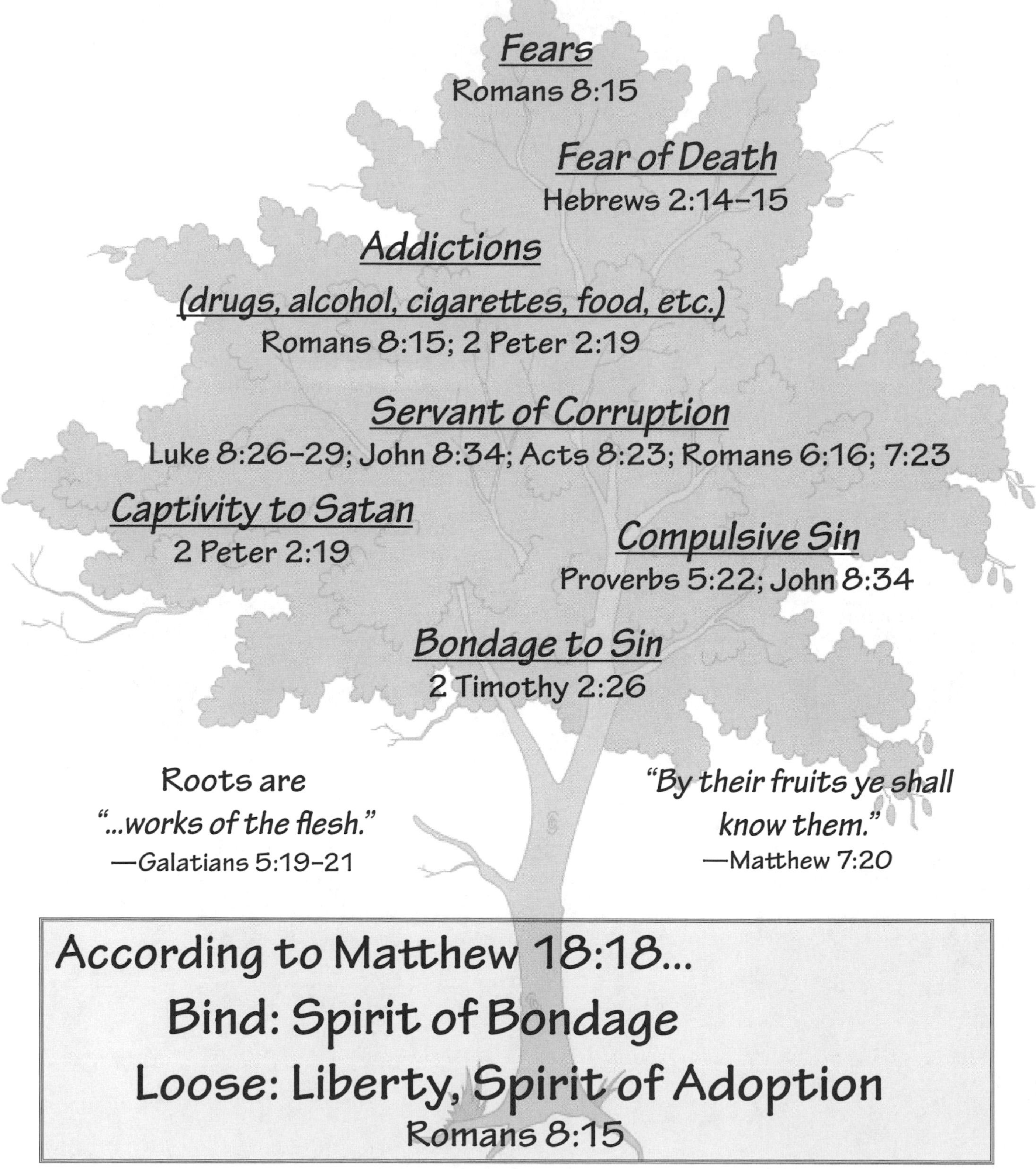

Fears

Romans 8:15

Fear of Death

Hebrews 2:14–15

Addictions

(drugs, alcohol, cigarettes, food, etc.)

Romans 8:15; 2 Peter 2:19

Servant of Corruption

Luke 8:26–29; John 8:34; Acts 8:23; Romans 6:16; 7:23

Captivity to Satan

2 Peter 2:19

Compulsive Sin

Proverbs 5:22; John 8:34

Bondage to Sin

2 Timothy 2:26

Roots are

"...works of the flesh."

—Galatians 5:19–21

"By their fruits ye shall know them."

—Matthew 7:20

According to Matthew 18:18...

Bind: Spirit of Bondage

Loose: Liberty, Spirit of Adoption

Romans 8:15

CHAPTER 11

Spirit of Bondage

This strongman usually works very closely with the spirit of fear, which we will consider in the next chapter.

"For ye have not received the spirit of bondage again to fear; but ye have received the Spirit of adoption, whereby we cry, Abba, Father" (Romans 8:15).

The Greek word, *"Abba,"* is a very personal word used in speaking to one's father. The modern equivalent for it in English would probably be our term of endearment, "Daddy."

In a normal family relationship, one of the most heartwarming times of the day is when the father returns home from work and his little boy or girl comes running up, crying, "Daddy, Daddy," and jumps into his arms. The father may be the director of a huge corporation or the president of the United States, but it doesn't matter; to the little child he is just plain "Daddy." That is the kind of relationship God longs to have with us—that of a loving Father gathering us to Himself, loving us with an everlasting love.

GET THE AUTHORITY

"Then said Jesus to those Jews which believed on him, If ye continue in my word, then are ye my disciples indeed; and ye shall know the truth, and the truth shall make you free" (John 8:31–32). We receive freedom to live life as it should be lived, without bondage of any kind, when we accept Christ as our Lord and Savior and believe His Word.

The sinner looks at that and says sorrowfully, "I can't accept Christ because there is so much I have to give up." And it is true the sinner must give up certain things. The mistake the sinner makes, however, is in the *value* he places on those things he must relinquish. A good illustration of this would be a fly, freshly caught and expertly wrapped up by a spider.

NOTES

NOTES

Total bondage does not happen in one day; it is a series of steps taken to satisfy the flesh.

The fly says, "At last I have a comfortable place to stay. See how the wind swings the web around like a big hammock. I don't have to waste my energy flying around anymore. This really isn't such a bad life."

"But friend," we remind him, "there's a huge spider that is about to have you for supper. When he gets done with you, all that will be left is a shell."

"No, this is a great life. Leave me alone. I'm happy living like this."

And the sinner swings back and forth, tightly bound by habits and addictions that keep him anchored on Satan's web. The end of it all for him is death, eternal separation from God and heaven.

Only as the light of God's Word reveals his true condition can the victim see that the little pleasure he receives isn't worth the price of staying on the web; that he needs to be freed from the terrible web of sin. When he cries out to the Lord, Jesus cuts him off the web in an instant. *Then* he sees what the situation was really like and sighs with relief, "I'm so glad to be free from Satan. How sweet it is to live for Jesus!"

Hold Fast Your Liberty

Paul told God's people to *"stand fast therefore in the liberty wherewith Christ hath made us free, and be not entangled again with the yoke of bondage"* (Galatians 5:1).

If there is anything more pitiful than seeing someone bound on Satan's web, it is to see that same individual crawl back up on the web after Christ has made him free. To have tasted of the freedom of God and then return to Satan's bondage is mind-boggling, but it happens. Why? Because *total* bondage does not happen in one day. It is a series of steps taken to satisfy the desires of the flesh until, suddenly, the individual realizes he is back on the web again and it is too late.

That is the reason we emphasize so strongly throughout this book the need of following the Word, not our feelings. If we are going to rule and reign with Christ, we must stop doing those things that lead us into bondage to the beggarly elements of this world system.

Addictions

Notes

Some of the manifestations of the spirit of bondage are: addictions of any kind, such as to drugs, alcohol, cigarettes, food, television, video games, pornography, and unnatural sex acts. The other extreme of addiction to food is anorexia nervosa (self-induced starvation). Rock music has an addictive quality that is destructive, in addition to the unwholesome message it usually spotlights. In short, as the name implies, anything that binds us so that we become involuntary slaves falls under the category of a spirit of bondage.

Alcoholism

Alcoholism is probably the most prominent and popular addiction in our world today. It is classified as a disease by some medical authorities, but God's Word does not support that diagnosis. Paul informed us in 1 Corinthians 6:10 that drunkards will not inherit the kingdom of God. The only reason God permits anyone to go to hell is because of their sin. So apparently God considers drunkenness to be a sin, not a disease.

The statistics relating to alcoholism are incredible.

- "Alcohol is the number two public health problem in America today, and it is getting more serious.
- "Ten million Americans are alcoholics and 20 million more are 'high risk' drinkers.
- "Seven of ten Americans use alcohol as a beverage.
- "One third of those who call themselves evangelicals drink alcohol, as do half of all ministers.
- It is "estimated that alcohol causes or contributes directly to 205,000 deaths each year in the United States.
- "Alcohol is a major cause of divorce, wife abuse, and child molesting."[1]
- "The cost to industry is estimated at $63 billion annually.
- "In the last ten years, 250,000 people have been killed in alcohol-related car accidents."[2]

NOTES

- "Alcohol is responsible for one-half of all homicides and one-third of all suicides."[3]
- "The life span of an alcoholic is shortened by 10–12 years."[4]

If alcoholism is a disease, it is the only one on earth that is spread by advertising. In spite of the terrible carnage, destruction, grief, and loss, alcoholic drinks are extolled on billboards, in magazines and newspapers, and on radio and television as a product that *everyone* should imbibe. If alcoholism is a disease, why don't the authorities stamp out the "virus" that causes it?

When polio was epidemic, the medical world swung into action and discovered a vaccine to halt the dreaded disease. But right now an even more virulent epidemic is raging, and virtually nothing is being done. "Every year 120,000 men, women, and children are crippled in wrecks caused by drunk drivers. For the most part our courts let most of the drunk drivers off with a slap on the wrist. Some drunks have been convicted repeatedly before they kill someone. Even drunk drivers who kill people often go without any meaningful punishment."[5]

Can you see them swinging in the breeze on Satan's web? And they think *we* are crazy because we don't like "spiders."

Note the statistic that one-third of those who call themselves evangelicals drink alcohol as do *one-half* of *all* ministers. Just reading the above statistics should convince any Christian that alcohol must be shunned as if it were a coiled rattlesnake. In fact, that was Solomon's advice in Proverbs 23:31–32, *"Look not thou upon the wine when it is red…At the last it biteth like a serpent, and stingeth like an adder."*

For those who rest their case on Paul's admonition to Timothy that he *"use a little wine for thy stomach's sake"* (1 Timothy 5:23), we would respectfully draw their attention to Paul's command in 1 Corinthians 5:11 not even to keep company or eat with a Christian who drinks to excess. And observe the list that Paul lumped them together with in verse 11: fornicators, covetous, idolaters, railers, and extortioners.

Anorexia Nervosa

Anorexia nervosa is a form of bondage that has only surfaced in the past few decades. Anorexics "have a low self-esteem and are especially sensitive to the many stressful changes of adolescence. They are usually compulsive exercisers and talk a lot about how fat they're becoming when they actually look like they're starving to death. Occasionally they step out of character and fall into a separate but definitely related ailment that is called bulimia, which is characterized by binge-eating and deliberate purging or laxative taking immediately afterwards."[6]

It is not necessary to go through *all* the manifestations of the spirit of bondage, but we do want to establish that it is extremely dangerous to get hung up on Satan's web. If you have tendencies toward this kind of behavior, please understand that God wants to deliver you and give you the freedom you desire.

Religious Bondages

We should also mention that many of the religious cults, such as the Unification Church of Sun Myung Moon, better known as the Moonies, the Hare Krishnas, the church of Scientology, and the Jim Jones-like organizations, as well as the more respectable sects, such as the Jehovah's Witnesses and Mormons, fall under this strongman.

Any practice, religion, or organization that uses fear to keep its members under control or that ties them to a set of rules contrary to the Word of God is usually inspired by the spirit of bondage. It is simple to recognize them because God offers us freedom not bondage.

The Fear of Death

The fear of death is a form of bondage, according to Hebrews 2:15. *"Who through fear of death were all their lifetime subject to bondage."*

I remember a lady in her 80s who was near death and petrified at the thought of it. I explained to her how Jesus could deliver her, and she accepted Him as her Savior. Then I rebuked the spirits of bondage and fear and loosed

Notes

God offers freedom, not bondage.

NOTES

Satan had the power of death, but Jesus took the keys.

health, strength, and resurrection life to fill her. I prayed that when her time came to die it would be peaceful and with such love that she would have no fear. Three days later, I learned she was up and about and had even been on some trips out of the house with her family.

Another lady was suffering with stomach cancer. She was just a tiny, frail, bedridden shadow. I prayed that the Lord would peacefully take her home, rebuked the spirits of bondage and fear, and asked the Lord to quicken her body. Several days later, she was out sweeping her walk.

About that time, I went to the Lord to find out what was going on; everyone I had prayed for to have a peaceful death was getting up, restored to health. He let me know that He was just allowing them to enjoy a few more months or years of life, free from bondage and fear, so they would have a taste of what His peace is like before going on to heaven. Isn't the Lord good?

You see, Satan *had* the power of death, but he doesn't anymore where Christians are concerned. When Jesus died, He descended into the place of the unrighteous dead and took the keys of hell and death (Revelation 1:18). Paul assured the believers that to be absent from the body is to be present with the Lord (2 Corinthians 5:8). There is nothing to be afraid of!

How About You?

That is what Jesus wants to do for you, too. It doesn't matter what your problem may be, Jesus is ready to set you free. The only thing we must be willing to do is give up the life of sin, acknowledge that we are sinners, and ask for God's pardon. Then the spirit of bondage can be bound once and for all.

Praying for Your "Impossible Person"

Each one of us has someone who is in such bondage to sin that we have all but given up on him ever being born-again. We have argued with him for so long he has tuned us out and turned us off. But don't give up! There is still hope!

When I pray for impossible people, I bind a spirit of bondage that is keeping them bound in their sins and loose the spirit of adoption (Romans 8:15) to begin working in them. It is the Spirit of the Lord that brings them to the point of decision. They still have their own free will in the matter, but the Holy Spirit draws them (heel marks and all!) to that moment of decision more quickly when the spirit of bondage has been shackled in their lives each day in the name of Jesus.

Jesus instructed us in Luke 10:2, *"Pray ye therefore the Lord of the harvest, that he would send forth labourers into his harvest."*

It may be impossible for us to be physically present to lead that person to the Lord; in fact, we may be half a continent away. But the Holy Spirit will lovingly confront that person over and over again with the truth. When the day of his salvation arrives, the Lord will be faithful to have the right person there to help them.

You will be able to rejoice with the angels of heaven because you were faithful in your intercession for his salvation. Some come quickly, and others are a little more stubborn, but be assured that all of heaven is honoring your prayers of binding and loosing. Bind the enemy in his life each time the Holy Spirit nudges you to do it until you see results. The Holy Spirit is a gentleman and is waiting for you to come into agreement with God's will in the individual's life before He starts His work. Out of ignorance, he is continually throwing the doors open. Each time you bind the strongmen in his life, they will be bound for a season and hindered in their influence. Don't forget to loose or release the spirit of adoption to continue His work of drawing him to Christ. The impossible person may have other strongmen operating in his life that you recognize, such as the spirit of error, etc., so bind them also and loose the positive side the Lord wants to work in him such as the spirit of truth, etc.

Prayer

"Dear Father, I come to You realizing that only You can free me from the web of Satan. Thank You for Your great love for me. I desire to call You 'Abba, Father' and feel Your arms of love wrapped around me so I won't have to seek love from alcohol or any of the other false hopes

Notes

NOTES

Satan has dangled before my eyes, promising so much and delivering so little. Forgive me of my sins. I promise to serve You the rest of my life.

"Satan, I rebuke you in the name of Jesus Christ of Nazareth and bind your spirit of bondage according to Matthew 18:18, which states, *'Whatsoever ye shall bind on earth shall be bound in heaven.'* I see you now as you really are: a spiritual 'spider' trying to bind and paralyze me with your cords of habits and bondage. I command you in the name of Jesus to leave me alone and never return.

"Thank You, Lord Jesus, for Your beautiful freedom. I loose the spirit of adoption in my life according to Matthew 18:18, which promises me, *'Whatsoever ye shall loose on earth shall be loosed in heaven.'* Help me to continue on forever in the freedom of Your Holy Spirit. I promise to read Your Word and walk by faith, not by sight or feelings, so that I can obey Your will for my life. Amen.

A Personal Exhortation

Once the enemy is bound in your life, as a believer you don't have to continue binding him. He is bound. Just remind him of it when he tries to come back and knock on your door again. If you stumble and fall for his deception again, immediately confront the situation with another prayer that binds his power from beginning again in your life. Praise the Lord that His Holy Spirit is such a faithful guardian that He quickly makes you aware of your problems so they can be taken care of in your life.

Notes

Spirit of Fear

2 Timothy 1:7

Fears, Phobias

Isaiah 37:7–8; 2 Timothy 1:7

Nightmares, Night Terrors

Psalm 91:5–6; Isaiah 54:14

Torment, Horror

Psalm 55:5; 1 John 4:18

Heart Attacks

Psalm 55:4; Luke 21:26; John 14:1, 27

Fear of Man

Proverbs 29:25; Jeremiah 1:8, 17–19; Ezekiel 2:6–7; 3:9

Fear of Death

Psalm 55:4; Hebrews 2:14–15

Anxiety, Stress

1 Peter 5:7

Lack of Trust, Doubt

Matthew 8:26; Revelation 21:8

Roots are
"...works of the flesh."
—Galatians 5:19–21

"By their fruits ye shall know them."
—Matthew 7:20

According to Matthew 18:18...

Bind: Spirit of Fear

Loose: Love, Power, and a Sound Mind

2 Timothy 1:7

Chapter 12

Spirit of Fear

For God hath not given us the spirit of fear; but of power, and of love, and of a sound mind.
—2 Timothy 1:7

Two Kinds of Fear

There are actually two different kinds of fear: positive and negative. Positive fear is a natural sort of protection that keeps us from hurting ourselves. We don't stick our hands in a blazing fire because we know it will do permanent damage to our bodies. We could characterize this fear more as a "deep respect."

I "respect" fire or electricity, so I obey their laws. The same principle applies to God. *"The fear of the LORD is the beginning of wisdom"* (Psalm 111:10). I obey God's commandments because I respect Him for who He is.

If the individual does not understand what is going on, a natural, positive fear can escalate to the point that a spirit of fear takes over. For example, an accident or great tragedy can be the trigger that causes a positive fear to balloon into negative fear, inspired and magnified by the strongman of fear.

We know a spirit of fear is at work when our spiritual vitality is affected. Negative fear chokes out faith, joy, peace, and love. It binds, paralyzes, and weakens the Christian and softens him up for the arrival of other spirits, such as infirmity and bondage. Medical science tells us that fear can cause many kinds of sickness.

In reality, negative fear is the negative "faith" of the devil. We believe what the devil says, more than God's Word, when we allow fear to reign in our life. Fear is directly opposed to God's laws. For this reason, *"the fearful, and unbelieving...shall have their part in the lake which burneth with fire and brimstone: which is the second death"* (Revelation 21:8).

Notes

NOTES

Fear is not from God.

Unbelief

Jesus pinpointed the disciples' fear while they were battling the storm as a lack of faith. *"Why are ye fearful, O ye of little faith?"* (Matthew 8:26). What were they afraid of? They thought they were going to drown. They didn't comprehend that it was Jesus who had control over death. He is Life! Isn't it strange that the very thing most people fear the most, death, is what they will eventually receive because they are fearful, *"the second death."*

Fear Came to Eden

The first appearance of fear in the human race came after Adam and Eve sinned. *"I heard thy voice in the garden, and I was afraid"* (Genesis 3:10). Do you suppose there is a relationship between sin and fear? In many cases there is. The sinner has every right to be fearful because he is walking in disobedience to God. Whenever the destroyer wants to pick him off, it is open season.

Love

John said, *"There is no fear in love; but perfect love casteth out fear: because fear hath torment. He that feareth is not made perfect in love"* (1 John 4:18). When Adam and Eve had perfect love, before they sinned, there was no fear of the animals or elements or even of God Himself.

The child of God who obeys God's Word should *never* permit fear to take him prisoner, especially when he is aware of the fact that fear is not from God. *"For **God** hath not given us the spirit of fear"* (2 Timothy 1:7, emphasis added). That means that you and I can refuse it in the name of Jesus because whatever is not from God isn't for us. The phrase, "Fear not," is mentioned in one form or another 365 times in the Bible—one time for every day of the year. We do not have to put up with fear for even *one* day.

Symptoms

Some of the major areas under the control of the spirit of fear are: phobias, nightmares, sickness, death, worry, excessive timidity, stress, psychological complexes, and heart attacks.

Heart Attacks

Scientists have discovered that highly emotional events, both good and bad, can upset heart rhythms to the point that sudden cardiac failure takes place. Jesus prophesied that this would be a sign of the end times, *"Men's hearts failing them for fear, and for looking after those things which are coming on the earth: for the powers of heaven shall be shaken"* (Luke 21:26).

We had a man in one of the Costa Rican crusades so dominated by fear that he had been a virtual prisoner in his own room for three years. God delivered him from the spirit of fear, and he resumed a normal life.

Job

The case of Job is used to show that it is God's will for *some* Christians to suffer sickness, loss of children, and untold agony. But according to Job's own words, the problem that initiated the whole episode was fear. *"For the thing which I* ***greatly feared*** *is come upon me, and that which I was afraid of is come unto me"* (Job 3:25, emphasis added). He opened up the door to satanic oppression by fearing the loss of his children, wealth, and health. When Satan asked for the opportunity to come against Job, he had a legal entry into Job's life, the open door of fear, and he took advantage of it with a vengeance. Up until that time, Satan hadn't been able to touch him because of God's hedge around him. Note that God still restricted Satan in his actions, even though He didn't stop him, until Job got his thinking straightened out.

Good Things Come from God

People say, "This is a classic example of the battle between good and evil, and Job happened to be the unfortunate pawn God used." But that is not characteristic of the just, loving, merciful God we serve. He does not casually throw us to the wolves just to prove some point, nor does He reward good people by giving them evil things. On the contrary,

> *Every good gift and every perfect gift is from above, and cometh down from the Father of lights, with*

Notes

NOTES

> *whom is no variableness, neither shadow of turning.*
> (James 1:17)

> *If ye then, being evil, know how to give good gifts unto your children, how much more shall your Father which is in heaven give good things to them that ask him? If ye then, being evil, know how to give good gifts unto your children, how much more shall your Father which is in heaven give good things to them that ask him?*
> (Matthew 7:11)

We had better hope that God doesn't treat us all like He supposedly treated Job, because then He would have to do the same thing to every overcoming believer. It certainly wouldn't be worthwhile for us to be more than conquerors if that was our fate, would it?

Job Shut His Open Door

No. When Job finally got things sorted out, *"the LORD turned the captivity of Job"* (Job 42:10). In other words, God released him from the captivity of Satan's fear. *"So the LORD blessed the latter end of Job more than his beginning....After this lived Job an hundred and forty years"* (verses 12, 16). Since many scholars believe that the entire book of Job took place in 9 to 18 months, we can see that when Job got the victory over fear in his life, he had 140 years of peace, prosperity, and a beautiful family. The devil never again had an open door to enter his life through fear.

My Victory over Fears

My personal battle with fear took place while we were missionaries to Nicaragua. I can trace it all back to a lack of trust in God and failure to read His Word as I should have done. We were living in Managua just prior to the earthquake and wars that have since taken place.

Our home was located in an area outside of Managua, where there had been a number of robberies with people being held at gunpoint or knifepoint. The thieves would hold the people captive for hours while they sacked the house. I didn't care so much about our household things as much as I worried about the safety of our two small children and myself. Jerry had to be gone every night to preach at the crusades in the city. Many times, I would stay home alone with the children until the wee hours of the morning without a telephone or car. Sometimes the electricity would go out, and we would be without lights until late into the night. For someone fresh from the United States, it was devastating.

The more I allowed fear to prey on my mind, the worse things got. I opened the door to a spirit of fear. I should have doubled my efforts to read the Word of God, but instead I slacked off. As a result, I was almost physically ill with worry and fear. All kinds of thoughts would go through my mind, and I felt no power in the Holy Spirit like I had before. I was finding it more and more difficult to express love in relationships. I just felt torn apart.

I would say to myself, "If my husband really loves us, why isn't he home more of the time? Why is he always gone? How can he leave us like this?" You see, if I would have just known what to call my attacker at that point and stood against him in the name of Jesus, I could have overcome that spirit by the power of the Word. But I had to learn many hard lessons before receiving healing and liberty. That is one of the reasons I began studying what the Word has to say about spiritual warfare. I wanted to know what was attacking me and how to stop it.

Praise the Lord, His Word showed me exactly what I had to do to have the victory. Now I am free, and I'll remain so as long as I continue following God's Word.

Since teaching this study, ladies have confessed to me that they were afraid to let their husbands go to work in the morning because of their fear that he would be injured or killed in an accident. They were afraid to let their children play in the yard because something might happen. They were afraid to love their husbands or other people for fear of being hurt by them. Do you know we cannot love our husbands, wives, children, or anyone else with complete abandon unless fear has been dealt with correctly in our lives? I could not even love the ministry God had called me to until I mastered fear in the name of Jesus.

NOTES

NOTES

Christ has delivered us from fear if we use His Word.

Nightmares

We can be free from fear even while we sleep. *"Thou shalt not be afraid for the terror by night; nor for the arrow that flieth by day"* (Psalm 91:5).

When our girls were young, they would have nightmares once in a while. So I taught them a paraphrased version of Psalm 56:3, "When I am afraid, I will trust in the Lord." They have mentioned so many times since then how that little verse helped them through many nights.

The truth of the matter is that a person is capable of thinking on just one thing at a time. When we bring every thought into captivity, as we are commanded to do in 2 Corinthians 10:5, we defeat the enemy. We reject his thoughts and begin to think on Scriptures or praises to God. Don't allow your mind to play with negative thoughts. Think on the good, the lovely, the good reports, etc. that Paul commanded us to think on in Philippians 4:8.

When my girls encountered big dogs or other terrifying circumstances on their way to school, they would repeat the verse in Psalm 56:3. It became an automatic response to danger. They knew the Lord was with them, and the fear would subside. Peace would come to their hearts. That is why we must program ourselves with the Word and then use it when the need arises. Quite often, the spirit of fear will take advantage of crisis times when we are the weakest to spring an attack on us. When that happens, we use the Word of God in an *aggressive* manner against fear. We repeat what God has said: "God hasn't given me a spirit of fear, so I rebuke it in the name of Jesus. I refuse to fear. Spirit of fear, go in the name of Jesus."

Fear: Is It Normal?

Someone may say, "Oh, it's normal to have fear. I've always been like that." Yes, it *is* normal for *sinners* to have fear, but not God's children. Christ has delivered us from fear, if we will just use His Word.

I would like to caution you not to view horror movies that can be used by a spirit of fear to bring terror into your life. Many people have said that movies, such as *Friday the 13th* and others that portray scary, twisted, evil things, were the open door for a spirit of fear to attack them. If you just observe the horrible previews on television of upcoming movies in the theaters, you will see how Satan is using this method to bind people with fear. And to think, they pay money for the "privilege" of being harassed by a spirit of fear!

NOTES

Phobias

Phobias, such as acrophobia (fear of high places), astraphobia (fear of lightning), claustrophobia (fear of enclosed places), hydrophobia (fear of water), nyctophobia (fear of darkness), pyrophobia (fear of fire), and thanatophobia. (fear of death), are all forms of the spirit of fear. Excessive timidity, worry, and psychological complexes that keep us from being free to express ourselves all have their roots in fear and must be destroyed if we are to be truly free to enjoy life as God intends.

People who are seeking the baptism of the Holy Spirit sometimes are attacked by a spirit of fear. It tells them they are not going to get the *real* Spirit of God but a counterfeit. God's Word plainly instructs us,

> *If a son shall ask bread of any of you that is a father, will he give him a stone? or if he ask a fish, will he for a fish give him a serpent? Or if he shall ask an egg, will he offer him a scorpion? If ye then, being evil, know how to give good gifts unto your children: how much more shall your heavenly Father give the Holy Spirit to them that ask him?* (Luke 11:11–13)

We get *exactly* what we ask for when we pray in the name of Jesus.

Let God's Word Be Your Guide

The best way to combat fear is to fill our hearts and minds with the Word of God and then use it like a sword against the fears of Satan. Chop them down to size—that's what a sword is for. Paul said, *"take...the sword of the Spirit, which is the word of God"* (Ephesians 6:17).

The last part of the verse that we started this chapter off with is a beautiful promise that God will give us

NOTES

everything necessary to overcome the enemy, *"God hath not given us the spirit of fear; but of* ***power****, and of* ***love****, and of a* ***sound mind****"* (2 Timothy 1:7, emphasis added). Take these things God has provided, and live in the freedom of His Love.

Fear Has to Go!

"Father, I see that fear is not from You. I understand that fear, worry, and doubt are the negative faith of the enemy. Forgive me for ever doubting Your ability to watch over and care for me. I will trust You from this time forth as my Source of security."

No More Attacks

"Satan, in the name of Jesus, I bind your spirit of fear according to Matthew 18:18, which says very clearly, *'Whatsoever ye shall bind on earth shall be bound in heaven.'* I will not stand for your attacks of fear. Leave me alone, this very instant, and never return. If you try, I'll use the sword of the Spirit against you."

Receive His Peace

"Thank You, Lord Jesus, for Your peace, power, love, and sound mind. I loose Your Holy Spirit in my life according to Matthew 18:18, which promises, *'Whatsoever ye shall loose on earth shall be loosed in heaven.'* I refuse to allow fear to rob me of all the good things You have for Your children. I claim the mind of Christ from this day forward. Thank You for delivering me from fear. Amen."

Notes

Seducing Spirits

1 Timothy 4:1

Hypocritical Lies

1 Timothy 4:1; Proverbs 12:22

Deception

Romans 7:11; 2 Timothy 3:13;
2 Thessalonians 2:10; 1 John 2:18–28

Attractions to/Fascination with False Prophets, Signs and Wonders, etc.

Mark 13:22

Seared Conscience

1 Timothy 4:1; James 1:14

Wander from the Truth

Deuteronomy 13:6–8; 2 Timothy 3:13

Seducers, Enticers

1 Timothy 4:1; 2 Timothy 3:13; Proverbs 1:10

Fascination with Evil Ways, Objects, or Persons

Proverbs 12:26

Roots are
"...works of the flesh."
—Galatians 5:19–21

"By their fruits ye shall know them."
—Matthew 7:20

According to Matthew 18:18...

Bind: Seducing Spirits

Loose: Holy Spirit, Truth

John 16:13

Chapter 13

Seducing Spirits

Now the Spirit speaketh expressly, that in the latter times some shall depart from the faith, giving heed to seducing spirits, and doctrines of devils.
—1 Timothy 4:1

These strongmen are especially active in the last days of our age, as evil becomes nearly irresistible. Their prime target is people who have accepted Christ as their Savior. Satan plays both ends against the middle. If he can't entice Christians with the usual sins, he uses false religions to entangle them. For varied reasons, these blood-washed believers depart from the faith and embrace religions invented by devils.

The Invasion

We are seeing an invasion in the United States of foreign, offbeat, demonic religions, and even one that brazenly states that it is the church of Satan. All of these religions will eventually culminate in the worldwide religion the false prophet will employ to elevate the antichrist to his position of world leader.

How exactly does Satan seduce a Christian? *"But every man is tempted, when he is drawn away of his own lust, and enticed. Then when lust hath conceived, it bringeth forth sin: and sin, when it is finished, bringeth forth death"* (James 1:14–15).

This is the identical tactic Satan used on Eve in the garden of Eden. The lure or temptation was dangled before her eyes by the Serpent. *"And when the woman saw that the tree was good for food, and that it was pleasant to the eyes, and a tree to be desired to make one wise, she took of the fruit thereof, and did eat, and gave also unto her husband with her; and he did eat"* (Genesis 3:6).

Only when she allowed her lust, or fleshly desire, to *respond* to the lure, did she sin. When the temptation moved into the action state, it became sin.

Notes

NOTES

Don't let Satan neutralize your effectiveness for God's work.

WEAKNESSES THAT OPEN DOORS

After the evil spirits have located the Christian's weaknesses of the flesh, they concentrate specifically in those areas. If the believer repents of his sin, God forgives him. But if he doesn't and he continues sinning, he opens himself more and more for the evil spirits to dominate his mind and body. He has left an open door that Satan interprets as an invitation to continue his activities.

Other related spirits may join the originals, and the Christian is bound more tightly until he finds it difficult to respond to God as he once did. His spirit desires to be free, but any effort to seek God brings him back around to the sin that is dominating his life.

NEUTRALIZATION

He is not *possessed* by a demon, but he is so harassed and oppressed by the sin and accompanying demonic activity that he is neutralized as far as any spiritual progress is concerned. I have seen Christians neutralized by sickness, economic problems, unsaved relatives, fear, heaviness, and spiritual pride, to name a few.

Let's suppose, for instance, that you ask one of these Christians about making a donation to missions. Their answer will immediately reveal the particular area where they are being dominated by the enemy. "Oh no, my finances are in terrible shape now. I would be afraid to make such a commitment. Besides, my husband is unsaved, and he wouldn't like for me to do that. And we have had a lot of sickness lately, so you know how it is."

This person is probably saved and wants to go to heaven, but she is so locked in place by things that normal Christians overcome by faith in God's Word that her effectiveness for God's work has been reduced to absolute zero. All she wants to talk about are *her* problems.

"But the things you mentioned don't sound so sinful to me," someone says, "economic problems, fears, unsaved relatives, and sickness." But listen carefully: they are sinful if they keep the person from doing what God wants them to do. Let's analyze why Mrs. Neutralized Christian has those problems. Her financial lack stems from an inability to control her credit card spending. Time after time, she commits the sin of "credit card," or spending more than she should on things she really doesn't need. Remember, Eve *"saw"* that the fruit was good for food and *"pleasant"* to the eye. Because of sin, Mrs. Neutralized Christian doesn't help the missions program, and souls go to hell because no missionaries were able to reach them with the gospel. I think that is serious, wouldn't you agree?

NOTES

Unsaved Relatives

We've already covered fear and infirmity in other chapters, so let's look at the last excuse—unsaved relatives. In a large number of cases where the husband or wife is not saved, it can many times be traced to some problem in the Christian partner's life. There are some Christian women who prefer that their husbands remain unsaved so they will have a ready-made excuse for any failure in their Christian walks. The whole situation blows up in their faces, however, when the unsaved partner, by some miracle, does get saved. Sometimes they spend the rest of their lives being a thorn in the now-saved partner's side.

The Carnal Christian

Most carnally-minded or neutralized Christians remain in an area of spiritual neutralization where they aren't happy either *in* or *out* of the church. Pity the poor pastor who attempts to shepherd such a church member for it is nearly impossible.

The carnal Christian will usually get his feelings hurt by something or someone and quit the church in a huff. Here is the point where many "depart from the faith." They are set up for the kill: living carnally, angry at the pastor or a fellow church member, but still having a desire to attend church. The seducing spirits swoop in with a modern, up-beat attractive religion, and Mr. and Mrs. Neutralized Christian are swept right into it before they can blink their eyes.

False Signs and Wonders

Other Christians are attracted by false prophets working false signs and wonders. *"For false Christs and false*

NOTES

When we follow signs and wonders instead of God's Word, we will have more trouble than we can handle.

prophets shall rise, and shall show signs and wonders, to seduce, if it were possible, even the elect" (Mark 13:22). When we follow signs and wonders instead of God's Word, we will have more trouble than we can handle. And the average Christian today is neglecting the reading and the hearing of the Word for a hundred different reasons. That makes them prime candidates for seducing spirits to exploit. Without God's Word to guide them, they are hopelessly astray.

Speaking of the false prophet who will operate during the Great Tribulation, we are told that *"he doeth great wonders, so that he maketh fire come down from heaven on the earth in the sight of men, and deceiveth them that dwell on the earth by the means of those miracles which he had power to do in the sight of the beast"* (Revelation 13:13–14). We are seeing the build up of that time in world history now. Only those who live carefully, according to God's Word, will be able to sense the true direction they should choose.

Music has a subtle, seducing affect on people who are unaware of its power. I am amazed at Christians who think nothing of listening to country and western, rock and roll, and even some popular music whose lyrics are laced with filth, adultery, occultism, drugs, homosexuality, and anti-God overtones. Their teenage children are allowed to frolic in that satanic cesspool as though it were nothing but harmless nursery rhymes. They wonder why their homes resemble padded cells at the state asylum for the mentally ill and their children want nothing to do with the things of God. My friend, we can't play in garbage and not end up smelling like trash.

Much of the music on the Top 40 charts has been written by witches and people actively involved in the occult. Some of the biggest hit records were not released until they were "blessed" in a witch's coven. They entreat demonic spirits to go with each record and be a direct influence on the minds and lives of the listeners. The seducing beat of the music is the same as that used in the jungles to conjure up evil spirits and cast voodoo spells. The latest trick is the use of backmasking to implant subliminal suggestions in the listeners' minds without them being aware of it.

Deception

Deception is the name of the game in these last days. Yet, believers are lined up at the theaters to see the latest offering of demon-inspired movies.

Paul warned Timothy,

> *In the last days perilous times shall come. For men shall be lovers of their own selves, covetous, boasters, proud, blasphemers, disobedient to parents, unthankful, unholy, without natural affection, trucebreakers, false accusers, incontinent, fierce, despisers of those that are good, traitors, heady, highminded, lovers of pleasures more than lovers of God; having a form of godliness, but denying the power thereof: from such turn away.... But evil men and seducers shall wax worse and worse, deceiving, and being deceived. But continue thou in the things which thou hast learned and hast been assured of, knowing of whom thou hast learned them; and that from a child thou hast known the holy scriptures, which are able to make thee wise unto salvation through faith which is in Christ Jesus.*
> (2 Timothy 3:1–5; 13–15)

The Key to Faith

The key to keeping the faith in these dangerous times is God's Word.

> *For though we walk in the flesh, we do not war after the flesh: (For the weapons of our warfare are not carnal, but mighty through God to the pulling down of strong holds;) casting down imaginations, and every high thing that exalteth itself against the knowledge of God, and bringing into captivity every thought to the obedience of Christ.* (2 Corinthians 10:3–5)

When we discipline our minds to think according to the way God thinks, it shuts and locks the door of our minds to Satan's temptation.

Also, it is a fact that our minds are capable of thinking on only one thought at a time. If Satan tries to interject his thoughts or temptations, it is then necessary to forcibly

Notes

The key to keeping our faith strong is God's Word.

NOTES

reject those thoughts and begin to think on the things of God. The Word directs us to think on the holy, the just, the good reports, the things of virtue, etc. We dare not let our minds drift into just *any* thought they happen to like or desire.

PRAYER

"Dear Father, forgive me for allowing the world to creep into my heart and life. I can see how deceptive the enemy is, and I know only Your Word can guide me through the spiritual minefields that lie ahead. I promise to read Your Word each day and seek Your guidance for my life.

"Satan, in the name of Jesus, I bind your seducing spirits according to Matthew 18:18, which says, *'Whatsoever ye shall bind on earth shall be bound in heaven.'* I realize you are trying to cause me to depart from the faith, so I command you to leave me alone from this moment on. I have chosen to follow Jesus, and that leaves you out, Satan. Go in the name of Jesus.

"Thank You, Jesus, for freeing me now from the evil spirits that were trying to deceive me. I loose Your Holy Spirit in my life according to Matthew 18:18, which tells me, *'Whatsoever ye shall loose on earth shall be loosed in heaven.'* I thank You for giving me the victory over every power of the enemy, and I appropriate the mind of Christ to be mine according to Your promises. Amen."

Notes

Spirit of Antichrist

1 John 4:3

Denies Deity of Christ
1 John 4:3; 2 John 7

Denies Atonement
1 John 4:3

Against Christ and His Teachings
2 Thessalonians 2:4; 1 John 4:3

Humanism
2 Thessalonians 2:3, 7

Anti-Christian
Revelation 13:7

Teacher of Heresies
1 John 2:18–19

Worldly Speech and Actions
1 John 4:5

Deceiver
2 Thessalonians 2:4; 2 John 7

Lawlessness
2 Thessalonians 2:3–12

Roots are
"...works of the flesh."
—Galatians 5:19–21

"By their fruits ye shall know them."
—Matthew 7:20

According to Matthew 18:18...

Bind: Spirit of Antichrist

Loose: Spirit of Truth

1 John 4:6

Chapter 14

Spirit of Antichrist

And every spirit that confesseth not that Jesus Christ is come in the flesh is not of God: and this is that spirit of antichrist, whereof ye have heard that it should come; and even now already is it in the world.
—1 John 4:3

Fundamental Attacks

This spirit attacks the very foundation of Christianity, the virgin birth of Jesus Christ. If Jesus was not God in the flesh, then all His other claims, such as the atonement, healing, the baptism of the Holy Spirit, the resurrection of the dead, the rapture of the church, and the Lord's second coming, are false.

The spirit of antichrist works through those who teach that Jesus was a good man, but nothing more. Muslims categorize Jesus as being a great prophet, but just one of many. Even the supposed messages from UFOs nullify the divinity of Christ.

Secular Humanism

Secular humanism has been labeled the most dangerous religion today. It typifies the ancient struggle between man's will and God's.

"Simply stated, humanism is a man-centered religion that mistakenly thinks it can solve the problems of man, independent of God.

"Dr. Bill Bright, national director of Campus Crusade for Christ...says: 'Have you ever wondered why our society is becoming more secular, why prayer and Bible reading are no longer welcome at our public schools?...Have you wondered why Americans are much more tolerant today of sexual freedom, homosexuality, incest, and abortion? The religion of humanism is largely responsible.'"[1]

Notes

NOTES

Those people the spirit of antichrist uses can be recognized by their choice of key words and phrases.

"Students in many secular schools are made to believe that they are not accountable to God, parents, pastors, teachers, or civil authorities. They are told, '...anybody's values are as good as anybody else's and whatever you choose will be right for you because you chose it.'

John Dewey

"It is shocking for some to learn that John Dewey, the father of 'progressive' education, was an atheist. He was the founder and first president of the American Humanist Association. He said, 'There is no God and there is no soul.'"[2]

Can we wonder why our children are tempted to doubt the basic concepts of God's Word when they are exposed to a daily diet of this kind of blasphemy?

John warned us, *"Who is a liar but he that denieth that Jesus is the Christ? He is antichrist, that denieth the Father and the Son"* (1 John 2:22).

"Whether or not they like to admit it, Humanist Manifesto I and II are to the humanists what the Bible is to us.

"Consider the following quotes:

- '...We believe,...that traditional dogmatic or authoritarian religions that place revelation, God, ritual, or creed above human needs and experience do a disservice to the human species.
- 'We find insufficient evidence for belief in the existence of a supernatural;...
- 'No deity will save us; we must save ourselves.
- 'Promises of immortal salvation or fear of eternal damnation are both illusory and harmful.
- 'There is no credible evidence that life survives the death of the body.'"[3]

World Opinion

This spirit of antichrist is actively shaping world opinion to accept the devil's counterfeit for Christ. John said that we will recognize those people this strongman uses by their choice of key words and phrases. Their speech patterns will give them away to those who know the Truth.

"They are of the world: therefore speak they of the world, and the world heareth [pays attention to] *them"* (1 John 4:5).

The world blithely accepts the latest program of Satan as though it were the greatest thing ever proposed. They never question evil—only good. When it was time for the "do your own thing" phase of the program to take effect, the loyal subjects of this world immediately began parroting it without question. But God's people know this is not the language of God's Word. We do *not* do our own thing; we obey the will of God. *"We are of God: he that knoweth God heareth us; he that is not of God heareth not us. Hereby know we the spirit of truth, and the spirit of error"* (verse 6).

Mark Them!

We are to judge their words by the Word of God and then mark them as being from this world's system, under the direction of Satan. If these people knock at our door with their "new" message of how to attain a higher level of consciousness, or any other doctrine, we are not to receive or even listen to them. John warned us not to even say, "God bless you," to those who abide not in the doctrine of Christ. *"If there come any unto you, and bring not this doctrine, receive him not into your house, neither bid him God speed: for he that biddeth him God speed is partaker of his evil deeds"* (2 John 1:10–11).

This may seem very harsh until we realize that millions of people are being deceived by these false, ungodly teachers. *"For many deceivers are entered into the world, who confess not that Jesus Christ is come in the flesh. This is a deceiver and an antichrist"* (verse 7).

I've known Christians who say to these people, "I won't take your literature because I don't believe that way. I have another way of looking at it, but God bless you anyhow." On the contrary, we should plainly tell them that what they are propagating is not the Word of God. Those who are truly seeking the truth may stop and listen if we are led by the Spirit of God.

We Are Powerful in Combat

We have been given tremendous power to turn this world away from the evil purposes of Satan, so we need

Notes

We have tremendous power to turn this world away from Satan's evil purposes.

NOTES

not be shy about it. That is why we are here: to combat the power of the devil with the greater power of God. *"Ye are of God, little children, and have overcome them: because greater is he that is in you, than he that is in the world"* (1 John 4:4).

When we uplift Jesus, who is *"the way, the truth, and the life"* (John 14:6), He says that He *"will draw all men unto"* Himself (John 12:32).

God's Word Stands Forever

"Dear Father, thank You for Your Word and Spirit that will guide me through the last, evil days of this age. I place my trust completely in You, O God. Your Word states emphatically that *'heaven and earth shall pass away: but my words shall not pass away.'* Thank You for that promise. Forgive me for ever doubting Your ability to take care of me.

"Satan, in the name of Jesus, I rebuke your spirit of antichrist. I will not be dominated by your evil strongman, because greater is He that is in me than he that is in the world (1 John 4:4). I am an overcomer in the name of Jesus. I bind your spirit of antichrist according to Matthew 18:18, which promises me, *'Whatsoever ye shall bind on earth shall be bound in heaven.'* You cannot operate in my life because the Greater One dwells within me."

God's Provision

"Thank You, Lord Jesus, for showing me the way, the truth, and the life. I can relax in You because You have provided for my every need as I cooperate with You, Your Word, and Your Holy Spirit. I loose Your Holy Spirit in my life according to Matthew 18:18, which says, *'Whatsoever ye shall loose on earth shall be loosed in heaven.'* Thank You, blessed Lord, for walking with me until the end of this age. Amen."

Notes

Spirit of Error

1 John 4:6

False Doctrines

1 Timothy 6:20–21; 2 Timothy 4:3;
Titus 3:10; 1 John 4:1–6

Error

Proverbs 14:22; 2 Peter 3:16–17; 1 John 4:6

Unteachable

Proverbs 10:17; 12:1; 13:18; 15:10; 12,32;
2 Timothy 4:1–4; 1 John 4:6

Unsubmissive

Proverbs 29:1; 1 John 4:6

New Age Movement

2 Thessalonians; 2 Peter 2:10

Servant of Corruption

2 Peter 2:19

Contentions

James 3:16

Defensive, Argumentative

(Defend "God's revelations" to themselves personally)

Roots are
"...works of the flesh."
—Galatians 5:19–21

"By their fruits ye shall know them."
—Matthew 7:20

According to Matthew 18:18...

Bind: Spirit of Error

Loose: Spirit of Truth

1 John 4:6; Psalm 51:10

Chapter 15

Spirit of Error

We are of God: he that knoweth God heareth us; he that is not of God heareth not us. Hereby know we the spirit of truth, and the spirit of error.
—1 John 4:6

This strongman operates best when there is an ignorance of God's Word. People do not deliberately set out to believe a false religion. They are swept into it because it *appears* to be the truth.

Mirages

People lost in the desert, with the sun blazing down, see mirages that have every appearance of being real, but in reality are either figments of their imaginations or tricks the elements play on them. Many lost travelers follow mirages to their death because what they are seeing is always just out of their reach as they stumble along, searching for water or a way out of the desert.

Our world is filled with spiritual mirages urging lost souls to follow them to the water of life they so desperately need. But unless they have a map to guide them, they will search in vain because the terrain is so deceptive.

Jesus cries out to these parched souls, *"If any man thirst, let him come unto me, and drink"* (John 7:37). Christ is the *only* source of living water in this world. False religions, doctrines, and philosophies *look* good, but alas, they are just mirages and cannot satisfy the inner thirst of man's spirit.

Jesus told the woman at the well,

> *Whosoever drinketh of this water shall thirst again: but whosoever drinketh of the water that I shall give him shall never thirst; but the water that I shall give him shall be in him a well of water springing up into everlasting life.* (John 4:13–14)

Notes

NOTES

We can bind the spirit of error and loose truth.

Jesus offers us eternal life if we will receive Him into our hearts and follow His Word.

SPIRIT OF ERROR

The spirit of error usually works together with other strongmen such as a lying spirit, spirit of antichrist, seducing spirits, spirit of heaviness, spirit of haughtiness, perverse spirit, familiar spirit, and spirit of divination.

People who are dominated by a spirit of error cannot see the error. If they could, they would not continue following it. Their minds have been so clouded by this strongman that they are absolutely convinced they are right and everyone else is wrong. So it is necessary to be very patient with them and give them the Word of God according to the dosage they can receive. It may be just a word the Holy Spirit will have us speak. Then the Spirit takes that word and uses it as a light to reveal the error in their lives. As the lights are turned on, each person is able to identify the error he has been pursuing.

We can also aggressively attack this spirit through our own private intercession. We can daily bind this strongman of error and loose truth into their minds and lives. Jesus is Truth; therefore we are really loosing Jesus to have a greater influence on them. Because they are constantly opening themselves up to error, we must be consistent in our binding and loosing until they commit their lives to Christ and renew their minds in the Word of God.

In our crusades in Latin America, the people will many times repeat the sinner's prayer for a month or more before they begin to understand what has taken place in their lives. Their hearts have been so darkened by centuries of witchcraft and false religion that the light seeps very slowly into their inner beings.

But what a joy to see the light of God finally penetrate into their hearts and see them light up like a light bulb has been switched on inside of them.

The more fanatically they served the devil's lies, the more fanatically they will follow Jesus. We must not be reticent in reaching out to those who seem beyond help. There is a spirit on the inside of them crying out for reality.

NOTES

During one of the crusades in Costa Rica, a man would drive by in his pickup truck nearly every night screaming obscenities, honking his horn, and generally making a nuisance of himself. This craziness went on for nearly three months.

We had been constructing a new church building during that time to house the new congregation when the rains came later on. A couple of weeks before we moved the crusade into the nearly completed church building, the wild man finally stopped his pickup truck long enough to listen to the Word of God. We didn't know that he was an alcoholic and that his business, marriage, and life were falling apart. But the light of God's Word pierced his alcohol-fogged soul, and he accepted Christ as his Savior.

For a while we missed the wild man's nightly visits until Luis finally testified that he was the one who had been screaming and honking his horn to disturb the services for the past few months. "But Jesus has changed me," he told the people. "I have been delivered from alcohol, and now I am a new creature in Christ Jesus!"

We hadn't done any of the electrical wiring in the new building yet. We just moved the string of light bulbs from the lot to the church auditorium. One night Luis asked to talk to me. "I'm an electrician by trade," he said, "and God has told me that I should do all the electrical installation in our new building." From that time on, Luis was our official electrician, and he wired all the large church buildings we constructed in Costa Rica, as well as the open-air crusade lots where the new churches actually began. There was nothing Luis would not do for the work of God. The last time I talked with him, he was preparing to enter the ministry.

Now I *look* for fanatics to lead to Jesus. They make tremendous Christians.

The New Age Cult

A cult type of organization that has come out into the open is the New Age movement. Their promise of a new age, however, is just the same old, worn-out lie of the devil wrapped in attractive tissue paper to deceive the world.

NOTES

The basic New Age error is a belief that Satan is the good force in the universe and God is evil.

Their "Great Invocation" appeared in the *Reader's Digest* on page 203 of the October 1982 issue, as well as many newspapers throughout the United States. The "prayer" spoke of the return of Christ to earth, but it was merely a subterfuge; in reality their christ is none other than the *anti*christ.

Can you see the trick of Satan? He is still trying to ascend to the throne of God. Because God's Word speaks so clearly about the antichrist appearing at the end of this age, Satan does a flip-flop; he comes disguised as the "Christ" to a world that is desperately in search of direction.

When this man, who they call Lord Maitreya, appears on the world scene, he is supposed to bring peace, love, and everything else the world needs. The fact is that, according to God's Word, the very opposite will happen.

"The New Age movement has announced through its various leaders, such as Alice A. Baily, David Spangler, and Marilyn Ferguson, its plans to take over the world. They are preparing and fully expect to establish a mandatory New World Religion in which Master 'Messiahs' will appear to adherents of all the major world religions to persuade them of the 'truths' of the New World Religion and its accompanying 'Revelation.'"[1]

BEWARE...

"Ye therefore, beloved, seeing ye know these things before, beware lest ye also, being led away with the error of the wicked, fall from your own stedfastness" (2 Peter 3:17).

The verse that follows gives us the secret of how to walk in the truth.

As we are led by the Holy Spirit, we help those who will listen so they can come into a knowledge of the truth. *"Brethren, if any of you do err from the truth, and one convert him; let him know, that he which converteth the sinner from the error of his way shall save a soul from death, and shall hide a multitude of sins"* (James 5:19–20).

The Word of God is our only foundation. Paul instructed Timothy to *"study to show thyself approved unto God, a workman that needeth not to be ashamed, rightly dividing the word of truth"* (2 Timothy 2:15).

"But grow in grace, and in the knowledge of our Lord and Saviour Jesus Christ" (2 Peter 3:18).

That means there is a right way and a wrong way to divide, or interpret, God's Word. The correct way is to understand that truth will not contradict itself. God cannot be evil; He is *always* good. Satan cannot be good, even though there are times he appears to be; he is *always* evil. If you probe the false religions and cults long enough with the Word, you will discover without fail their basic error. Satan just cannot help himself. He is so twisted that when the light of the Word is shown on him, he will always reveal himself for what he is: a thief, a liar, a killer, and a destroyer.

NOTES

God cannot be evil;
He is always good.

The Scorpion and the Frog

The story is told of the scorpion and the frog who were on the bank of a river. The scorpion asked if he could ride across the river on the frog's back. The frog said, "Oh no, when we get to the middle you will sting me, and we'll both drown."

"That would be foolish of me," replied the scorpion. "I'm smarter than that. This is why I'm asking you to carry me; so I won't drown."

After a time, he convinced the frog of his good intentions, and they began their journey.

When they arrived at the middle of the stream, the frog proved to be a prophet. The scorpion couldn't resist the urge to sting the frog.

"Why did you do that after promising me you wouldn't? Now we're both going to die."

"I'm sorry, frog," answered the scorpion sorrowfully, "it's just my nature to sting."

Satan's Basic Nature

When we understand that the basic nature of Satan is to destroy and the basic nature of God is to bring life, we will be well on the road to understanding God's Word.

NOTES

Accept Christ as your Savior, allow the light of God's Word to illuminate your path, follow the direction of God's Holy Spirit, and you will *always* know the truth and the truth *will* set you free. (See John 8:32.)

Prayer

"Dear Father, thank You for giving me a firm foundation to build my life upon. In this world, so full of lies and deception, I can rest upon the truth of Your Word. Forgive me for trusting in myself. I place my life completely in Your hands. Forgive me of all my sins. I accept Jesus Christ as the Lord and Savior of my life, and I promise to live according to Your Word from this moment on."

No More Error

"Satan, I bind your spirit of error in the name of Jesus, according to Matthew 18:18, which states, *'Whatsoever ye shall bind on earth shall be bound in heaven.'* I refuse to follow your twisted ways and thoughts. I command you to leave me alone now in the all-powerful name of Jesus."

My Desire Is Truth

"Thank You, Jesus. I love You with all my heart, and I desire to serve You with all that is within me. I loose Your Holy Spirit of truth in my life, according to Matthew 18:18, which tells me, *'Whatsoever ye shall loose on earth shall be loosed in heaven.'* I thank You for helping me to be more than a conqueror. Amen."

Chapter 16

Spirit of Death

Although the spirit of death is not mentioned specifically by name in the Bible, there are a number of indications that death is more than just a condition or term.

Death and Hell

Revelation 20:14 tells us that *"death and hell were cast into the lake of fire. This is the second death."* John was not speaking symbolically of *"hell"* in this passage; it is a place that actually exists. It would seem, therefore, that *"death"* here means more than a mere definition of the last stages of killer diseases or fatal accidents.

The Last Enemy

Paul mentioned that *"the last enemy that shall be destroyed is death"* (1 Corinthians 15:26). In Revelation 20:10, we are shown the line of events that will take place at that time: *"The devil that deceived them was cast into the lake of fire and brimstone, where the beast and the false prophet are, and shall be tormented day and night for ever and ever."* Then comes the great white throne judgment of the unrighteous dead, when they will be rewarded for theirs sins. Only *after* that time will death and hell be cast into the lake of fire. So a definite distinction is made between the devil and death in these passages. Of course, death is under the direction of Satan, but according to this description it would seem that death is some kind of "being," possibly a powerful fallen angel.

Revelation 9 begins with the account of a bottomless pit that is opened by an angel of God during the fifth trumpet judgment or plague. Strange looking locust-scorpion type creatures stream up out of the pit to sting the ungodly for a period of five months. The torture of the sting is so terrible that the people will prefer to die, but *"death shall flee from them"* (verse 6).

Notes

NOTES

THE DESTROYER

These supernatural insects have *"a **king** over them, which is the **angel** of the bottomless pit"* (verse 11, emphasis added). This evil angel's name in Greek is *Apollyon,* which translates, "destroyer." He is still locked up in the bottomless pit, but the whole passage reveals that there is apparently a class of fallen angels whose chief work is to take life from the members of the human race who have fallen prey to accidents or disease.

Now let us go back to the exodus of the Israelites from Egypt. Many Christians believe that God killed the firstborn children whose parents had not placed the blood of a lamb on the doorposts of their home. But Exodus 12:23 puts a different light on the situation when read in conjunction with the above reference to the "destroyer.: *"For the LORD will pass through to smite the Egyptians; and when he seeth the blood upon the lintel, and on the two side posts, the LORD will pass over the door, **and will not suffer*** [permit] ***the destroyer** to come in unto your houses to smite you"* (emphasis added).

Paul had something to say on this subject also. *"Neither murmur ye, as some of them* [Israelites] *also murmured, and were destroyed of the **destroyer**"* (1 Corinthians 10:10, emphasis added).

It is important to understand that God wasn't the villain in Exodus; He was the only One with the power to keep the demonic destroyer from killing every firstborn child—or for that matter the whole family—whether there was blood on the doorpost or not. The "death angel," as this destroyer has come to be called, was not an agent of God, but of the devil.

Paul told us, *"Forasmuch then as the children are partakers of flesh and blood,* [Jesus] *also himself likewise took part of the same; that through death he might destroy him that **had the power of death**, that is, the devil"* (Hebrews 2:14, emphasis added).

That means that now we can shout along with Paul after we have accepted Christ as our personal Savior, *"O death, where is thy sting? O grave, where is thy victory?"* (1 Corinthians 15:55).

What does all this mean? If we are blood-washed children of God, we can stand against death in the name of Jesus as the Holy Spirit directs us, and death can be stopped from doing its deadly work. It means that those who have placed their trust and faith in God's Word do not have to fear death because Jesus has performed surgery on death and taken the stinger out, as far as His followers are concerned. Understand now that all of this is dependent upon the fact that the child of God knows his rights according to God's Word and applies them if and when the situation demands and as the Holy Spirit prompts him.

Are you saying then that Christians will never die? Spiritually, yes—physically, no. Should Jesus tarry, we will all eventually die physically. What this means is that death cannot attack us *prematurely,* just as God kept death from taking those Israelites who had placed the lamb's symbolic blood on their doorposts. There are actually Christians who are tricked by the deceiver into believing their time has come to die or are snatched away in an accident when, in reality, God isn't through with them yet.

A doctor friend of ours in Latin America had such an experience one day as he and his wife were returning home after a day of relaxation. An approaching car took his half of the road out of the middle, and our doctor friend had to swerve toward the ditch to avoid a head-on collision. As the case is in many countries around the world, there are usually people walking along the roads of this small Central American country, and, in missing the oncoming car, he hit a young girl walking along the shoulder of the road, throwing her some distance from the point of impact.

He and his wife scrambled out of the car in a state of shock and ran over to where the girl lay. She displayed all the signs of death, and it seemed useless to even try to treat her medically. At that moment, he testified that the Holy Spirit prompted him to rebuke the spirit of death in the name of Jesus, which he did with authority. Immediately the color returned to the girl's cheeks, and she started to get up, saying she was all right.

The doctor was amazed at her rapid recovery—there were just some cuts and bruises—and to their immense

NOTES

Christians never die spiritually.

NOTES

Death for a believer should be a promotion to a higher rank.

relief, they were able to take the girl home alive instead of in a coffin. Not only had death been robbed of a victim, but Satan was defeated in his attack on a child of God. The doctor was spared the trauma of taking an innocent child's life through no fault of his own, as well as all the legal hassles that would have ensued because of his status as a foreigner.

True, *"it is appointed unto men once to die"* (Hebrews 9:27), but that appointment should be according to God's calendar, not the Enemy's. Satan is a murderer, thief, and liar. He not only attempts to rob us of our salvation, health, children, peace, and finances but also our *years* on this earth to be Christian witnesses. *"Ye are of your father the devil, and the lusts of your father ye will do. He was a murderer from the beginning, and abode not in the truth, because there is no truth in him. When he speaketh a lie, he speaketh of his own: for he is a liar, and the father of it"* (John 8:44).

Let me stress once again that we must be very sensitive to the fact that it is God's Spirit speaking in such a situation, not ours. Once that is decided, you will find that when the faith or unction of God springs up in your heart or spirit *you will know it without a doubt.* Speak to death as you would any other spirit from the devil, but also remember to loose the spirit of life into the one you are praying for.

Christians Die by Faith

When and how should a Christian die? A Christian should die as differently from a sinner as light is unlike darkness. Death for the believer should be a promotion to a higher rank, not a fear-filled, trauma-laden tragedy. The Old Testament patriarchs called their children around the bed, prophesied over them, then simply gathered their feet up into the bed and yielded up their spirit.

I heard recently of an elderly Christian man who announced to his children at a family gathering, "I'm going to die at 3:00 p.m. tomorrow afternoon. I want you all to be there because I have something special to tell you before I go."

The children and grandchildren were shocked and cried, "You can't mean this, Grandpa. We don't want you to die!" But he insisted that it would take place as he said.

The next morning no one mentioned anything about what had happened the night before, and the aged grandfather played games, joked as usual, and seemed the same as ever. But just before 3:00 p.m. he said, "Oh, it's almost time. Come on everyone into the bedroom." He laid down on the bed and spoke, telling how he wanted them to live after he left them, and at 3:00 p.m. he entered the presence of the Lord as gently as if he had taken a heavenly elevator.

Jesus said in the parable of the rich man and Lazarus that angels carried Lazarus into Abraham's bosom, the abode of the righteous dead before Christ's death and resurrection. (See Luke 16:22.) After Jesus rose from the dead, He took the keys of hell and death with Him. (See Revelation 1:18.) Because of that victory, the Christian now goes directly to heaven after death. *"Therefore we are always confident, knowing that, whilst we are at home in the body, we are absent from the Lord: (**For we walk by faith, not by sight**:) We are confident, I say, and willing rather to be absent from the body, and to be present with the Lord"* (2 Corinthians 5:6–8, emphasis added).

Not only do we live by faith, but we must *die* by faith. Why do Christians fight and strain to stay on this earth when God's time has come for them to pass on to the place Jesus has prepared for them? Could it be they lack faith and actual knowledge of God's Word? Since they are unsure of their rights in God, they fear the unknown just as the sinner does.

But this need not be. God's Word is very clear. If we have accepted Christ and are living according to His Word, death no longer has power over us. Just as Jesus defeated death, so will we also, if we use the Word He has placed in our hands.

"Death and life are in the power of the tongue" (Proverbs 18:21). Speak the Words of God, believe God's Word, act on what God has said, and live by the Words of God. When it is time to step over into the next world, the Holy Spirit is perfectly capable of advising you that you have arrived

NOTES

Not only do we live by faith; we must die by faith.

NOTES

at the "going home" phase of your life—that time when the angels come to take you where sorrow will be obliterated and you will be in the very presence of our Lord and Savior Jesus Christ.

David, speaking of God, penned these words under the inspiration of the Holy Spirit, *"Precious in the sight of the LORD is the death of his saints"* (Psalm 116:15). We are not merely numbers to God. Just as we help ease our children over difficult areas of their lives, so God will be with us to help us through the last mile of this life.

Do not allow Satan to rob you of the years God has given you to live and then believe God for a peaceful home-going. That is the heritage of God's children, *not one minute before* or *one minute after* He calls us into His presence.

> *I call heaven and earth to record this day against you, that I have set before you life and death, blessing and cursing: therefore choose life, that both thou and thy seed may live.* (Deuteronomy 30:19)

Satan tries to deal a deathblow to all areas of a Christian's life. If he can't take the believer's life, then Satan will try to kill his finances, marriage, friendships, family relationships, etc.

You, the believer, can take your place of total authority in Christ Jesus and bind the enemy. Begin to back him away from what is rightfully yours. Speak words of life into every situation.

Jesus said, *"I am the way, the truth, and the life"* (John 14:6). When we are following Him, speaking the truth and life of the Word into an area of our lives, we are loosing the power of Jesus into it. His power can change anything!

Begin to walk in a closer daily relationship to God, and He will direct your steps. Sensitize yourself to the quiet voice of the Holy Spirit. *"But righteousness delivereth from death"* (Proverbs 10:2).

Run for the Prize: Achieve Your High Calling

"Dear Father, I choose Life to reign supreme in my spirit, soul, and body from this day on.

"Satan, I rebuke you and your spirit of death. You would try to destroy me, but you have already been condemned to the lake of fire. I refuse your destruction and robbery. Leave me now in the name of Jesus!

"Lord Jesus, thank You for Your spirit of life that indwells me and blesses everything I put my hand to do. I know I have authority to bind and loose according to Matthew 18:18. You stand behind Your Word to perform it in me. I glorify You and praise You for Your great mercies to me. Amen."

NOTES

Notes

CHAPTER 17

Additional Advice for Spiritual Warfare

NOTES

WORKS OF THE FLESH

Let's look at the fifth chapter of Galatians to know exactly what we are referring to when we speak of the "works of the flesh."

> *Now the doings (practices) of the flesh are clear—obvious: they are immorality, impurity, indecency; idolatry, sorcery, enmity, strife, jealousy, anger (ill temper), selfishness, divisions (dissensions), party spirit (factions, sects with peculiar opinions, heresies); envy, drunkenness, carousing, and the like. I warn you beforehand, just as I did previously, that those who do such things shall not inherit the kingdom of God.*
>
> (Galatians 5:19–21, AMP)

Other Scriptures that relate further works of the flesh are: Romans 1:28–32; Ephesians 5:3–6; 1 Corinthians 6:9; 2 Timothy 3:2–5; and Revelation 21:8.

Wherever the works of the flesh are *practiced,* there will usually be strongmen present, because that is their area of operation. Whether the works of the flesh get beyond that stage and into demonic activity depends on the individual involved. Many times, the first stage of the works of the flesh is curiosity, which leads to the initial participation. As the person is charmed and fascinated, the Holy Spirit is still present, in the case of Christians, to convict him of his wrongdoing. But if he ignores the conviction of the Holy Spirit over a period of time, which varies according to the person and situation, he may be in danger of initiating demonic activity because he has allowed an opening in his defenses through his continued sin.

NOTES

If we keep our defenses solid, we can live in the world untouched by evil.

THE HEDGE

"And whoso breaketh an hedge, a serpent shall bite him" (Ecclesiastes 10:8). This had to do with a special kind of hedge that was planted around the house to keep dangerous snakes from coming on the premises. If a break or opening was allowed in the hedge, the possibilities of a snake getting in were high. If snake were common in the area, it would happen sooner than if the house were not located in snake country. In other words, if we leave an open door in our spiritual hedges, the possibilities are high that we will be bitten.

But if we keep our defenses, or hedges, solid, we can live in this snake-filled world and never be touched by evil. Only the ministry of the Word of God by the Holy Spirit can keep us free from sin. If we avoid the Word on a daily basis, we shut off the alarm system, allowing the door to crack open so Satan can take a shot at us. We find ourselves in a battle we could have avoided.

Here is some additional advice to help in spiritual warfare.

USE DISCERNMENT

Not every problem in our spiritual lives is caused by a demon. Many times the problem begins because we step out of line with God's Word. Be careful to make your daily decisions according to God's will for your life.

QUIETLY TAKE DOMINION

Do not force your spiritual diagnosis on those who will not listen. Just quietly continue taking dominion over the situation in the name of Jesus, either within your own spirit or audibly when you are alone, until such time as the individual or the Holy Spirit indicates that he is ready to listen. The only exception to this rule would be a clear case of possession in which the Holy Spirit leads you to take direct action and cast it out. Then you must be careful to make sure the person is filled up with the Word and the Holy Spirit *after* the demons leave so that they cannot return in force at a later date.

A Greater Truth

Do not become so demon-conscious that you forget the far greater truth that your name is written down in heaven. (See Luke 10:20.) Be aware of your spiritual power as you act in the name of Jesus, but emphasize the positive as much as possible. God saves, heals, and baptizes in the Holy Spirit, and does all the truly great things in this world. Grow in the Word so the fruits of the Spirit can flourish in your life and the gifts of the Spirit can operate through you as the Spirit wills.

Give God the Glory

Always take time to give God the glory publicly for everything that is accomplished of a positive nature. Never touch the glory for yourself; it belongs to God.

Prayer Language

By all means, use your prayer language in spiritual warfare. (See Romans 8:26.) When we don't know how to pray, the Holy Spirit does. He will make intercession for you.

Use an Audible Voice

It helps to bind and loose according to Matthew 18:18 in an audible voice, when possible. Although Satan has the power to place temptations in your mind, he is still not able to read your mind. He can only see what your reaction is to the temptation by your resulting actions and words. That is why it is a good habit to speak the Words of God no matter how you feel or think. Only God is omniscient, which means He knows everything, including your thoughts (1 Kings 8:39).

I like to let Satan know audibly that he isn't fooling me by his tactics; that I refuse to do things his way and in fact am turning the Holy Spirit loose on him, according to God's Word, for even attempting to beguile me in the first place with his phony offers.

An Angel of Light

Remember that Satan can appear as an angel of light. (See 2 Corinthians 11:14–15.) Just because it looks good

Notes

NOTES

doesn't mean it is. *"But though we, or an angel from heaven, preach any other gospel unto you than that which we have preached unto you, let him be accursed"* (Galatians 1:8).

Stay Humble

We are not to be filled with pride because we are used by the Holy Spirit to help free people from the enemy's attack. *Any* believer, according to Mark 16:17, should be able to take dominion over demons in the name of Jesus. That is why we've made this study: to take the spookiness and spectacular out of dealing with Satan and get it on a level any layperson can handle who is a believer.

We should become so comfortable with the knowledge that we are the conquerors that we do not even worry about demons. When they stick their heads up, we recognize their symptoms and take dominion over them in the name of Jesus.

The important fact is that Jesus rules and reigns in our lives. Because of our relationship with Him, we have His power.

No Need to Fear!

There is no need to fear that demons will reach out and grab us as we pray for people. (See Luke 10:19 and Isaiah 54:17.) Our dominion over the realm of Satan is *complete*. The *demons* are the ones who fear *us* because we are God's children. James told us that demons tremble because they know what the situation really is (James 2:19). He said, *"Resist the devil, and he will flee from you"* (James 4:7). The word *"flee"* in the Greek translation means to run from something or someone in *terror*. The demons are terror stricken when we use the name of Jesus according to God's Word.

The only exception to this would be a bystander who is not a believer or someone who is unsure of his position in God. For this reason, we recommend that in spiritual warfare only Spirit-filled believers who understand that they are overcomers in the name of Jesus our Lord be present.

Walk by Faith

Do not wait for a physical confirmation to prove that something has happened. Nothing may happen on the surface, but a great spiritual process has been set in motion the moment we utter God's Word in faith. The victory is *always* ours. When Jesus cursed the fig tree, it died immediately, *but from the roots up.* It took time for the results to surface. (See Mark 11:20–21.) We walk by faith, not by sight.

Use Authority

Speak to the enemy in a normal voice of authority. It isn't necessary to scream. The less sure the person is of the Word, many times, the louder he shouts, as though he were trying to frighten the devil with his loud voice. The only thing that frightens the devil is Jesus Christ.

A Fact of Life

Spiritual warfare is not an elective; it is a fact of life. Some Christians erroneously believe that the moment a person accepts Christ he will never have to deal with demonic attack again because Jesus defeated Satan when He died and rose from the dead. If that were true, then why did Paul tell Timothy to *"fight the good fight of faith"* (1 Timothy 6:12).

Paul also said, *"Put on the whole armour of God."* Why? *"That ye may be able to stand against the wiles of the devil. For we wrestle not against flesh and blood, but against principalities, against powers, against the rulers of the darkness of this world, against spiritual wickedness in high places"* (Ephesians 6:11–12). He says, *"We wrestle,"* and then he lists the power we have at our disposal to win the wrestling match: truth, righteousness, gospel of peace, faith, salvation, Word of God, and praying in the Spirit. (See verses 14–18.)

True, Jesus won the battle over Satan, but we must *maintain* that victory on a daily basis in our own lives.

We were saved when Jesus died on the cross, but we are still to, *"work out* [our] *own salvation"* (Philippians 2:12). There is a daily part to our salvation that we are responsible for maintaining.

Notes

The victory is ours, even though the results may take time to see.

NOTES

WE ARE VICTORS!

One thing we can all agree upon is that Jesus has given us the victory over the power of the enemy, whatever his form of attack may be.

We realize not everyone will agree with the fact that demons have specialized areas of responsibility such as we have listed in this book, in spite of the fact that the Bible does mention them very clearly. We would just say that angels have specialized duties, so why wouldn't Satan's counterfeit kingdom? The above-mentioned Scripture in Ephesians 6:12 seems to also bear out this fact.

BINDING AND LOOSING

The prayer of binding and loosing at the end of each chapter is not intended to be the total extent of our prayers; it is merely the starting point. As you pray, interject your own needs and words into the prayer so that it becomes individualized to your particular needs. The prayer we have is merely an outline to help those begin who might not know where to start.

There is also solid evidence in the Greek translation of the Bible to substantiate that Matthew 18:18 belongs in the arena of spiritual warfare not only for church discipline, but across the board in dealing with the deception of the devil.

No one doubts that Jesus was talking about spiritual warfare in Matthew 12:29 when He said, *"How can one enter into a strong man's house, and spoil his goods, except he first bind the strong man? and then he will spoil his house."* The word *"bind"* in Matthew 12:29 is the same Greek word Jesus used in Matthew 16:19 and Matthew 18:18 when He said, *"Whatsoever ye shall bind on earth shall be bound in heaven."* (s.v. G#1210 in *Strong's Concordance of the Bible,* "deh'-o").

Further, the Greek language structure that is used to describe what we are to bind in the three Scriptures above does not refer to the binding of persons, but of things who have no gender form—they are neuter. *("They neither marry, nor are given in marriage; but are as the angels which are in heaven"* [Mark 12:25]). That would have to be the case in the binding of Satan and demonic spirits because spirits are not masculine or feminine—they are neuter. *They are the things we are to bind—not people!*

Second, the word, *"whatsoever"* in Greek is *ho,* which is the neuter singular in Matthew 16:19 and, *hosa,* which is the neuter plural in Matthew 18:18. So the reading of Matthew 16:19, which is identical, and Matthew 18:18 would be, *"Whatsoever* [not masculine or feminine in gender] *ye shall bind* [not masculine or feminine in gender] *on earth shall be bound in heaven"* (page 1288, *The Hebrew-Greek Key Study Bible,* Spiros Zodhiates, Th.D).

Even in English, when referring to people, we say, "*who*soever" and in referring to things, as the case is here, we say "*what*soever."

Therefore it is perfectly clear that Jesus was speaking about prayer and spiritual warfare in Matthew 16:19, 18:18, and 12:29.

The Greek word used here for *"loose"* is *luo.* The primary meaning is, "to loosen (literally or figuratively)" (s.v. G#3089 Strong's Concordance of the Bible), which is what we are doing figuratively when we "loosen," or allow, permit and cooperate with what the Holy Spirit chooses to do in the situation.

God Is Always Greater

The forces of God are overwhelming in comparison with the evil forces. Sometimes, in a study of this kind, it appears that the only forces working in this world are evil. That is why I like to balance this study out with a series on the positive works of God. God doesn't give us power just to *fight* against the devil. We are here to establish His kingdom on this earth. We have the gifts of the Spirit and the fruit of the Spirit. There are twice as many good angels as bad ones.

A good example of this would be the time Elisha prayed that his servant would see the situation as it actually appeared, even though the city was surrounded by the horses and chariots of the king of Syria. *"Lord, I pray thee, open his eyes, that he may see. And the Lord opened the eyes of the young man; and he saw: and, behold, the mountain*

Notes

We are here to establish God's kingdom on earth.

NOTES

was full of horses and chariots of fire round about Elisha" (2 Kings 6:17). It wasn't even a contest. So it is necessary to keep our spiritual understanding in proper perspective.

Continue to Grow Spiritually

Now that we have been freed from the power of the enemy, we should go on to the bigger and better things that God has for us. Dig out the precious promises of God's Word. Progress in the things of the Spirit. Walk with God. *"Press toward the mark for the prize of the high calling of God in Christ Jesus"* (Philippians 3:14). God has crowns and rewards waiting for those who faithfully accomplish His will in their lives. The greater One lives within us!

Go and Teach...

Jesus said,

> *All power is given unto me in heaven and in earth. Go ye therefore, and teach all nations, baptizing them in the name of the Father, and of the Son, and of the Holy Ghost: teaching them to observe all things whatsoever I have commanded you: and, lo,* ***I am with you alway, even unto the end of the world****.*
>
> (Matthew 28:18–20, emphasis added)

Notes

Notes

End Notes

Unless otherwise indicated, all Scripture quotations in this study are from the King James Version of the Bible.

Chapter One

1. *The Random House Dictionary,* s.v. "divination."
2. *Miami Herald;* October 19, 1975; page 12.
3. *The New Bible Dictionary;* Eerdmans; page 766.
4. John Newport, *Demons, Demons, Demons;* Broadman Press.
5. *The New Bible Dictionary;* Eerdmans; page 767.

Chapter Two

1. *Reader's Digest;* July, 1965; page 260.
2. *Bantam Books;* pages 173–174.
3. Noel Langley, Hugh L. Cayce, ed.; *Edgar Cayce on Reincarnation;* Warner Books; page 271.
4. Thomas Sugrue, *The Story of Edgar Cayce: There Is a River;* Dell Publishing Co., Inc.; page 304.
5. *Edgar Cayce on Reincarnation;* pages 271–272.

Chapter Three

1. *Dake's Anotated Reference Bible, New Testament;* page 170; note "n".
2. *National Enquirer;* March 15, 1983; page 61.

Chapter Five

1. *Newsweek;* April 18, 1983; page 80.
2. *Statesman Journal;* Salem, OR; January 20, 1987; page 1.
3. *Statesman Journal;* Salem, OR; September 19, 1983; page 1A.
4. *Statesman Journal;* Salem, OR; January 20, 1987; page 1.

Chapter Seven

1. A. Snider, *Pentecostal Evangel;* April 17, 1983.
2. Jane S. White, AP writer, *Statesman Journal;* Salem, OR; February 3, 1981.

Chapter Eleven

1. Dr. K. S. Kantzer, *Christianity Today;* Sept. 18, 1981.
2. *Parade Magazine;* May 1, 1983; page 16.
3. *The Denver Post;* June 6, 1974; page 12.
4. *Time Magazine;* April 22, 1974; page 59.
5. U.S. Sen. J. A. Denton Jr.; *National Enquirer;* March 29, 1983; page 51.
6. *Star;* March 22, 1983; page 6.

Chapter Fourteen

1. Tim LaHaye, *Charisma;* May, 1983; page 31.
2. *Christian School Comment;* Vol. 12, No.5.
3. *Charisma;* May 1983; page 32.

Chapter Fifteen

1. Constance Cumbey, *The Hidden Dangers of the Rainbow;* Outline, page 5.

Notes

About the Robesons

Drs. Jerry and Carol Robeson were missionaries to Latin America for twenty years. They ministered in Nicaragua, Costa Rica, Paraguay, Jamaica, Mexico, and Chile. They specialized in open-air crusades that were held every night in an area of the city where a new church was needed. One crusade church in Costa Rica, for example, has more than ten thousand people in attendance.

The Robesons maintained an active television and radio ministry. They produced and directed more than twelve hundred Christian television programs in Latin America and the United States, and many hundreds of radio broadcasts. They also appeared as guests on television programs all over the United States.

Jerry and Carol graduated from Northwest College in Kirkland, Washington, and Vision International University in San Diego, California, where they each earned a Ph.D. in theology in 1996.

Jerry died September 18, 1999, leaving his wife, Carol, with two married daughters and four grandchildren. Until 1999, the Robesons were both very active in teaching seminars in the United States and Latin America. Carol continues on with this ministry of seminars and retreats.

Carol is the owner of Shiloh Publishing House, located in Keizer, Oregon. She has authored *God's Royal Road to Success; Mighty Warriors, Jr. Activity and Coloring Book;* and *Dynamic Faith of the Believer.* With her husband, she coauthored *Strongman's His Name...What's His Game?* and *Strongman's His Name...II.*

For information, contact:
Dr. Carol Robeson
P.O. Box 100
Woodburn, OR 97071
1-800-607-6195

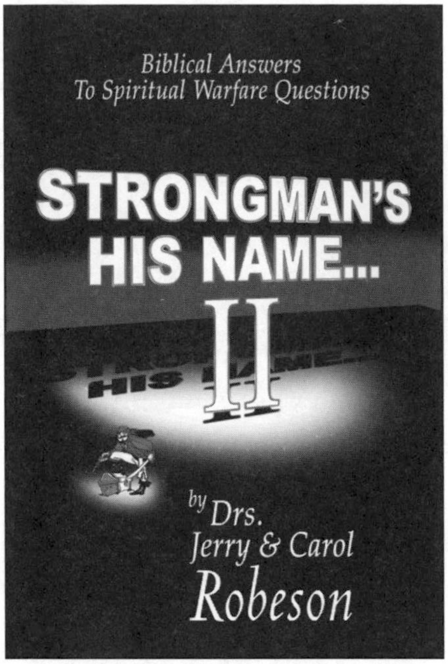

Strongman's His Name...II

Drs. Jerry and Carol Robeson

Why do I have so much trouble with the devil if he's already defeated?
How can I tell the difference between God's voice and the enemy's?
Is there really a spirit of Jezebel?
I've prayed, so why are things worse?
Can Satan read my mind?

Questions about spiritual warfare—we all have them, but often we don't know where to find the answers. In these instructive pages, Jerry and Carol Robeson share with you the principles of prayer and spiritual warfare that will give you the power to survive and thrive. Their simple, no-nonsense, biblical answers will help you understand what it means to be one of God's warriors in these last days.

ISBN: 978-0-88368-603-4 • Trade • 256 pages